# ALL ABOUT
# CARPETS

*Everything You Need to Know*
*A Consumer Guide*

Second Edition

# GLENN REVERE

**RFI**
**PUBLISHING**

Published by RFI Publishing

Book Design by Monkey C Media
www.MonkeyCMedia.com
Edited by Lynette Smith

Front cover photograph courtesy of Gulistan Carpets

Printed in the United States of America

Revere, Glenn.
    All About Carpets: Everything You Need to Know, A Consumer Guide / Glenn Revere. --2nd Ed.-- San Diego, CA: RFI Publishing, c2013.
    p. ; cm.
    ISBN: 978-0-9888882-3-4 ; 978-0-9888882-4-1 (ebk)
    Includes glossary. Includes index.
    Summary: What every consumer needs to know about carpets: carpet options, types of carpet, buying carpet, cleaning carpet, carpet warranties. Revision of the 1988 edition issued by Tab Books.

    1. Carpets--Handbooks, manuals, etc. 2. Rugs--Handbooks, manuals, etc. 3. Carpets--Care. 4. Carpet laying. 5. Carpet backing. 6. Rug and carpet industry. I. Title.

TS1775.5 .R48 2013
677/.643--dc23                                    1307

This book is dedicated to my wife and best friend, Eileen.
She encouraged me to write the original *All About Carpets*
many years ago. Then she encouraged me again
when it was time to write this current version.
This book would not have happened without her.

# *Acknowledgments*

I wish to thank and acknowledge many people, some alive and some not. I want to thank the people at The May Company–Cleveland who hired me out of college 43 years ago as an Assistant Buyer and put me in the carpet department. Then I must thank Carpet Technical Service for originally training me as a carpet inspector 40 years ago.

Thanks also to the many carpet retailers and manufacturers who have used my services all these years. I must also thank the Institute of Inspection, Cleaning, and Restoration Certification (IICRC) and their many instructors for their ongoing education classes. They truly help maintain a high level of professionalism in our industry.

Some individual instructors who tirelessly gave their time and knowledge over the years: Mike West and Carl Williams of West & Williams and Lou Sweigart of L & N Services.

My thanks to Gulistan Carpet for my book-cover photograph; to Leggett & Platt for the carpet-pad photographs; to Richard King of KFC Inspections for his invaluable help with the installation chapter; and to Casa Interiors for allowing me to photograph in their store.

And a special shout-out to my neighbor and fellow author, Jody Catlin. Jody encouraged me to join Publishers & Writers of San Diego. By joining this outstanding group, I met scores of local folks in the publishing business and many local authors who inspired me to finish my manuscript. I also met the Monkeys!

My gratitude list would not be complete without mentioning the Monkeys! No, not the band—my book team at Monkey C Media: Jeniffer Thompson, Chad Thompson, Julio Pompa Frizza, Aleta Reese, Amy Sheinberg, and Matt Gross, and my copyeditor Lynette Smith. Thank you for your ideas, your help, and your enthusiasm!

# CONTENTS

# PREFACE

I wrote the original *All About Carpets: A Consumer Guide* almost 25 years ago to answer your questions and save you money. A lot has changed since then. I have expanded the scope of this book to not only save you money but help you understand your choices and answer the questions you might not even know to ask. Do you have questions about how the carpeting in your home was installed? Or how to make sure that your new carpet will be installed the right way? Or do you have cleaning or maintenance questions about carpet?

Quality carpeting costs a lot of money. You want to get the most for your hard-earned cash. That's why it is so important to understand what you are buying, how carpet is made, what your warranty covers, and what different types of materials are used. If you have gone into a floor-covering store and felt confused by competing claims and fast sales pitches, then this book is for you.

Over the years, many people have asked me the same basic questions. They've been frustrated trying to find the right answers. People also have been confused because they get different answers from "experts." Ask the same question to a salesperson, installer, or cleaner and see if you get the same answer three times! While these people have valuable field experience, few of them are trained in all areas of floor covering.

This book was written for you, the consumer, to help you select your residential carpeting. (Commercial and rental properties have different carpeting needs.) Flooring is one of the largest investments most people make, after their home and car. All too often, when a person buys flooring, a decision is based on very little hard information. You can find lots of information about cars, appliances, computers and so forth; however, little non-technical material is available for consumers looking for practical advice about carpeting.

The brochures published by the industry are a good start. But some are little more than propaganda for a particular product. Most are sketchy at best. When *All About Carpets* was published in 1989, it was the first non-technical carpet book written for the public. Today, *All About Carpets: Everything You Need to Know, A Consumer Guide* is still the only consumer-oriented book of its kind. It is for people who want to make smart decisions regarding carpeting and the related areas of underlayments, installation, and maintenance. This book also answers questions about carpeting performance. It helps you understand what to expect from your new carpets. As a flooring inspector, I show you effective ways to complain to retailers and manufacturers about defects, installation shortcomings, and other problems. Plus, you'll understand terms used by the industry when you read through the extensive glossary.

I've left two subjects out of this book. The first concerns price as related to quality. Everybody wants to save money. But, as I explain, there are so many variables regarding flooring prices that it is almost impossible to easily equate price to quality. A low price does not always mean a bargain. It can also mean a cheaply made product. A high price does not always mean the best quality. It could mean a rip-off. When you read this book, you'll learn so much that you'll recognize a bargain when you see one. That is how *All About Carpets: Everything You Need to Know, A Consumer Guide* will save you money.

The second subject is about the "best" carpet. Let's get this straight: There is no such thing as the "best" carpet. There are many great carpets made from well-engineered fibers. One of them is "best" for you. But so many variables go into choosing a carpet—performance, style, color, budget—that *you* are the only one who can decide on the "best" carpet for your home.

## A LITTLE HISTORY

Twenty-five years ago, flooring was all about carpeting. The carpet industry had 300 carpet mills. Today there are fewer than twenty independent manufacturers. The most familiar names are now divisions of a few big mills. Warren Buffet owns the largest producer, Shaw

Industries. Besides carpet, Shaw produces wood, ceramic tile, and laminate flooring. Today, flooring is about carpet, wood, and laminate. But, depending on the area of the country, carpeting still makes up a large part of a home's overall floor coverings.

Twenty-five years ago, most carpet was sold by department stores: Sears, the May Company, and similar large national department stores sold the bulk of floor coverings. Specialized flooring retailers were practically a footnote. Today, department stores have abandoned the flooring business. Specialty and home improvement stores are where you go to buy flooring for your home now.

Twenty-five years ago, I had 15 years' experience in the carpet industry. I was a carpet cleaner and a carpet inspector with a lot of experience, but I was not a Certified Carpet Inspector. Today, I am a Certified Flooring Inspector with specialized training in carpet, wood, laminate, and vinyl flooring inspections. I have changed the name of my company from Professional Carpet Inspections to Professional Flooring Inspections to reflect my expanded knowledge. I have certifications in carpet cleaning, repair, and installation. I also understand how subfloors, such as concrete and wood, affect what's installed over them. I know how a given type of flooring must be installed.

Twenty-five years ago, carpet fiber—nylon, acrylic, polyester, polypropylene—was made only from petroleum-based oil. Carpet pad (except for felt) was also made only from petroleum-based oil. Today, some nylon fiber is made from recycled nylon carpet. Most polyester fiber is made from recycled soda bottles and bottle caps. Some is also made from soybean oil. And some carpet underlayment is now made from soy-based oil.

Twenty-five years ago, personal computers and the Internet were in their infancy. It was difficult for someone outside the industry to get any information about carpeting except from a salesperson. Today, the Internet gives you a flood of information with a couple of keyboard taps. But it can be overwhelming to sort and catalog all that information for accuracy. And then, when you walk into a store with your research, there is a good chance the salesperson will say things that will confuse you! How do you compare products when a lot of stuff is private labeled? How do you know something is really "on sale"? How can you tell if warranties are meaningless?

This updated book is the best way to answer your questions and eliminate all the confusion so many people have about carpets. This book was written to help consumers make smart, more satisfying decisions. I want people to be happy with their carpeting and its performance. At the same time, I will tell you the secrets, scams, and scuttlebutt that the industry doesn't want you to know. I actually had an industry executive tell me that I shouldn't write this book. He said, "Consumers shouldn't have too much information. It's too confusing." Can you imagine that? Let's see if he was right; here we go!

# INTRODUCTION

A little history always puts things into perspective. The origin of rugs has been traced to the beginning of civilization itself. Archeologists studying the Tigris-Euphrates area, considered the birthplace of civilization, have found evidence of rugs dating to 2500 BC. These rugs were probably woven from grasses and reeds or were made from animal skins. As the early civilizations learned to spin cotton and wool, these fibers found their way into the weaving of rugs, as well as clothes.

As civilizations expanded, the use of rugs spread. The walls of Egyptian tombs more than 3,000 years old show pictures of rugs. The oldest rug in the Cairo museum dates to about 1800 BC. Wool rug weaving developed into an art in areas now known as Turkey, Iran, India, and China. When people discovered how to spin silk into thread, silk also became incorporated into rug weaving. The first oriental rugs came from these areas of the world.

The Greeks learned to use fine rugs when they conquered the Persians and Turks. The Romans derived their appreciation of rugs from the Greeks. In fact, *carpet* comes from the Latin verb meaning "to card wool." When the Turkish empire grew to include north Africa, Spain, and southern France, rug weaving spread to these areas.

But the art of rug weaving was perfected in China and India between AD 500 and AD 1200. The royal families made great use of fabulous rugs woven from gold, silk, and jewels. Marco Polo brought fantastic tales of beautiful rugs back to Venice after his travels to the Orient. At about the same time, weaving appeared in Moslem-controlled areas of Spain and was firmly established in the area by AD 1300.

Woven rugs are traced to England as early as the tenth century, but the few that were made were strictly for the kings and their castles. These fabrics were more like mats than what we would call rugs. Most people continued using straw mats over dirt or stone floors. With the royal blessing, the weaving trade began in England around 1350 and spread to France 100 years later, when the first French guild for rug weavers was formed.

Another 100 years were to pass before Queen Elizabeth brought Persian weavers to England and firmly established the craft in Europe. England's damp climate created a demand for wool rugs, and what started as a fashion whim by royalty soon spread to the populace. By 1700, a sizeable rug-weaving industry was located around the town of Wilton, England. Other craftsmen quickly started a weaving center in the town of Axminster, England. By the middle of the eighteenth century, rugs were in widespread use throughout the cultured world.

Floor coverings came to this country with the first settlers. In fact, oriental rugs were prized possessions of the Pilgrims, as were hand woven rugs from Europe and England. Those who could not afford such luxuries used deer or bear pelts on the floors. Straw mats were also popular in colonial times. They were cheap and easy to make, and the natural fibers needed were found up and down the Eastern seaboard. In the spirit of the "waste not, want not" ethic, rag rugs made from scraps of discarded clothing or other textiles were hooked and braided to grace the floor of many early homes. Some beautiful examples are found at the Smithsonian Institution's American History Museum in Washington, DC.

But rug weaving by hand, while one of the oldest ways to make carpet, is slow and tedious. In 1800, a good team of weavers could make only six to eight yards of carpet in a 12-hour day. So rugs were affordable only to the rich. Around the same time in France, Joseph Jacquard invented a device for hand looms that predetermined the placement of colored yarns. By using a series of punch cards similar to a player piano, the Jacquard loom repeated the same pattern over and over. Changing the order of the cards or using different cards changed the pattern. This loom greatly increased production. Also around the same time, Americans set up a carpet-weaving center in Philadelphia to make a 27–inch-wide fabric that was sewn into carpets of varying width. These fine products gave Philadelphia an excellent reputation and made the area the center of American carpet manufacturing.

Around the middle of the nineteenth century, Erastus Bigelow invented the first steam-powered loom and eventually combined it with the Jacquard mechanism. After inventing a power loom to make wider carpet, Bigelow began his own mill in Massachusetts. He then refined his inventions and licensed his machines to other manufacturers, and the carpet industry gradually moved from Philadelphia to New England.

Carpet production increased rapidly and price decreased to where factory-made carpeting was available to many more people. Production from one loom soon jumped to 75 yards a day! Gradual improvements allowed more types of weaves, and made them more quickly.

More improvements were made after the American Civil War. Power looms were modified to make not only the Brussels weave (a modified loop pile) of the earlier power looms, but Axminsters, Wiltons, and others. Carpets became ever more popular over the next 50 years, but the basic manufacturing techniques did not change much until the introduction of tufted carpeting.

The idea of a tufted fabric originated during the 1920s with the quilters and bedspread makers living in the northern hill country around Dalton, Georgia. A widely used device was actually a modified sewing machine that stitched, or tufted, the designs and embroidery work into a bedspread. The early carpet tufting machines were modified bedspread tufters and were designed to make carpet 27 inches wide—the standard for woven carpet.

After World War II, the demand for housing increased dramatically, and so did the demand for carpet. Manufacturers looked for faster, more economical ways to make carpet. The tufting machines were quickly improved to make carpet in several widths, including 9-foot, 12-foot, 15-foot, and 18-foot widths. Tufted carpet became really popular in the early 1950s when quality carpet was offered at a price nearly everyone could afford. With a choice of several widths, an installer could fit most rooms with very few seams. Today, most carpet is available in only a standard 12-foot width. With modern tools and equipment, an experienced installer can piece together 12-foot goods so that seams are generally not noticeable.

# 1

# HOW FLOOR COVERINGS ARE MADE

Machine-woven carpet is very close in quality to handmade carpet. But now computer operated, machine-powered looms are modified in many ways to produce intricate colorations and patterns not possible with hand looms. Woven carpet is much more expensive than tufted carpet because the manufacturing process is slower. Also, the pile is generally heavier and is often woven from wool or wool blends instead of synthetic fibers. While woven carpet makes up less than two per cent of the residential market, it has attractive features including strong construction and a wide range of colors and designs.

## WOVEN CARPET

*Axminster, Wilton,* and *Velvet* are the three major types of weaves made today. For all practical purposes, any of these three weaves will give excellent service and many years of enjoyment. The differences between Axminster, Wilton, and Velvet are illustrated in Figures 1-1, 1-2, and 1-3.

The back of all woven carpet (Figure 1-4) is made by interweaving lengthwise and crosswise yarns to form the backing and face yarns simultaneously. In order to grasp the workings and differences of the various types of weaves, you must first understand a few terms. (See the Glossary for more terms.)

*Heddle:* A frame that holds warp yarns lengthwise, across which are drawn the weft yarns. The frame moves up and down to make an opening through which the shuttle passes with the

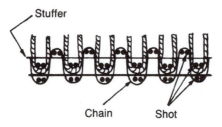

Figure 1-1. The side view of an Axminster weave carpet.

Figure 1-2. The end view of a Wilton weave carpet.

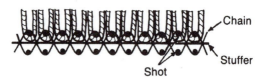

Figure 1-3. The side view of a Velvet weave carpet.

weft yarn. This mechanical action is the same as the over-and-under movement of a hand loom.

*Pick:* Weft yarns that run between the warp yarns. The higher the number per inch, the tighter the weave.

*Pitch:* The number of lengthwise warp yarns in a 27-inch width of fabric. The higher the number, the finer the weave.

*Shot:* The number of widthwise weft yarns in relation to each row of pile yarns that help form the backing. Measured by the number of shots per inch, a higher number indicates a heavier carpet.

*Shuttle:* The long, narrow device that carries the weft yarns across the loom when the heddle opens.

*Warp:* Yarn that runs lengthwise down the loom.

*Weft:*   Yarn that runs widthwise across the loom.

*Wires:*   Metal strips inserted in the weaving shed in the Jacquard and Velvet weaves so that the surface yarns are bound down over them forming a loop of the proper height. Round wires are used in loop pile fabrics and the loops are left uncut as the wire is withdrawn. Flat wires with knife edges are used in Wilton, Velvet, and Saxony weaves and the loops are cut as the wire is withdrawn, producing a fabric with a plush finish. The number of wires to the inch lengthwise is an indication of quality.

All fabric weaving methods are similar. A loom is actually a frame with crossbars at each end. Lengthwise yarns are stretched between pins in the bars. These warp yarns run between slots in the heddle. The shuttle then passes through these slots with the weft yarns. As the frame moves up and down, it carries the warp yarns that bind with the weft yarns. Each time the heddle goes up or down, another row of fabric is formed. The *reed* is a comb-like device that pushes each weft row against the preceding one to ensure a tight fabric.

To make carpet, a backing is formed along with the pile. The lengthwise part of the back is made by warp yarns called *chain* and *stuffer*. More than one chain can be used to bind the weft yarns in order to make a stiffer, heavier fabric. First, the chain (warp) yarns are threaded through wires fastened to the heddle and move with it. Second, the chain is wound on a cylinder above the loom and unwinds as the heddle moves. Next, the face warp yarns are fed into the loom separately by a framework of *creels* to create the face pile. The face yarns are looped over wires that are perpendicular to the warp yarns. The thickness of the wire determines the pile height. Finally, the face warp yarns are woven into the backing yarns by shots of weft yarn. When the wires are removed, looped pile is formed. For cut pile, a knife is attached to the far end of the wire. When the wire is withdrawn, the knife cuts the loops. Patterned carpet is made using combinations of varying pile height and/or cut and loop face yarns.

Even by machine, weaving carpet is a slow, tedious process. It takes a long time to set up the hundreds of creels that a loom requires. Once the loom is set up, the weaving process is relatively slow. Combine the slow manufacturing process with more costly yarns like wool or wool blends, and it adds up to a more expensive carpet. Fortunately, the quality makes up for the added expense.

Woven carpets are heavy, thick fabrics that seem to wear forever. It would be difficult to select a poorly made woven carpet. They are a high quality investment that enhances any home.

## TUFTED CARPET

The vast majority of carpet sold today is *tufted*. A tufting machine is a giant sewing machine with as many as 1200 needles across the 12-foot width. Like a sewing machine, each needle stitches yarn supplied by a cone on creel racks into what becomes part of the finished carpet. A fabric known as the *primary backing* is fed by a roller system under the rows of needles. The needles puncture the backing and stitch the yarns into it. The yarn enters from the back to the front of the primary backing and is tufted in lengthwise and upside down. The distance between the needles is the *gauge*, or tightness of rows of yarn, and is one indication of carpet quality. The closer the rows, the tighter and heavier the fabric (Figures 1-4 and 1-5).

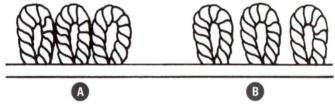

**Figure 1-4. High density (A) and low density (B) looped-pile carpet.**

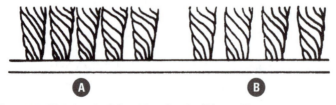

**Figure 1-5. High density (A) and low density (B) cut-pile carpet.**

The *stitch rate* counts the number of tufts per inch in a length of face pile. The stitch rate relates to the density of the pile. The closer the stitch, the heavier the carpet. A stitch rate of seven to eight tufts per inch makes a heavier carpet than a stitch rate of four to five tufts per inch, for example.

*Gauge* is measured in rows per inch of width of face pile. For example, good quality carpet is often 1/10th gauge, meaning that there are 10 rows of tufts per inch across the width. Gauge is the same as pitch in woven carpet. Most common gauges are 1/8th and 1/10th, or 8 and 10 rows of yarn per inch, respectively.

The diameter of the tufted yarns will, to a certain extent, determine the closeness of the needles. A thick cable yarn cannot be tufted as closely together as a fine yarn, simply because of its physical dimensions. Therefore, gauge is only one of several factors used to determine carpet quality. Generally, a good quality carpet will have the rows tufted as closely together as possible. This is important on carpeted stairs. Stair noses (the outside edge of the stair tread) are curved. The carpet pile will *grin*, or spread apart, along the curve. If the carpet gauge is too wide, you will see the carpet backing along the stair nose.

Once the carpet yarn has been tufted into the primary backing, it is called the *face yarn*. The rows of face yarn sometimes run in straight lines or sometimes follow a zigzag, or *stepover*, stitch. The type of stitch is not important for the grade of carpet. It primarily has to do with the type of equipment used, the pattern the designer has in mind, and the finished texture of the carpet.

Tufting machines are computer guided and can easily be programmed to produce varying results. The amount of needle penetration determines the length of the face yarns, commonly known as *pile height*. Normal tufting operations produce only looped pile, the same stitch used in garments (Figures 1-6, 1-7, and 1-8). Varying the pile height makes carved or scrolled patterns. To make cut-pile or plush fabrics, a knife is fitted to the tufting mechanism. As the loop of yarn is pushed through the primary backing, a knife hooks the loop and cuts it, forming two cut tufts from one loop. By tufting in two loops with one needle, four cut tufts are stitched in for an even heavier fabric. To make a patterned carpet, the carpet pile can have both cut and uncut loops. Pile height helps create the overall "look" of the finished carpet. Shorter tufts are used in more formal designs; longer lengths, like shag, are more informal.

*Density* is the combination of stitch rate, gauge, and pile height. For the most part, shorter-face piles stitched closely together make a more dense carpet. The more dense a carpet, the better it tends to hold up.

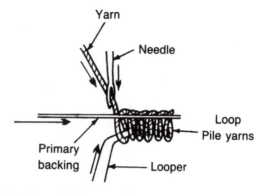

Figure 1-6. Tufting looped-pile carpet. Stage one.

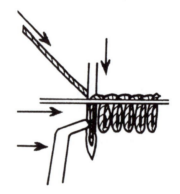

Figure 1-7. Tufting looped-pile carpet. Stage two.

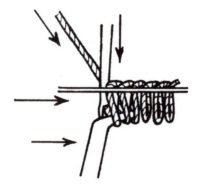

Figure 1-8. Tufting looped-pile carpet. Stage three.

# CARPET BACKINGS

The *primary backing* is the backbone of the finished carpet. Primary backings were made from jute fiber many years ago. Today, they are all made from woven polypropylene. Polypropylene, also called olefin, is made from oil and is essentially a type of plastic. The material used for primary backings is either *woven* or *non-woven*. Non-woven primaries look like a thin felt, very flat and uniform in texture and thickness. For woven primaries, flat threads called *slit film* are cut from a thin sheet of olefin. Then the flat threads are woven together, making the finished material into a mesh. The face yarns are tufted into the backing fabric and form the pile.

Manufacturers have a steady supply of olefin. In addition, the fiber is inert. It is hydrophobic. This means it is unaffected by water. It will not swell up in water, nor will it rot in water. Outdoor carpet (like synthetic grass) with olefin backings withstand all types of weather. Indoor carpet with olefin backings resist flooding, urine, and other types of water damage. Mildew won't form because the synthetic fibers are not a food source for the mold that makes the mildew.

Once the fibers dry out, the carpet returns to normal. If the face yarns are synthetic, they will also resist water damage. The latex-rubber bond between the primary and secondary backings might be weakened by the water, depending on the formula of the latex. If the bond is weakened, the primary and secondary backings will separate. This is called *delamination*. Once delamination occurs, the fabric wrinkles and bubbles because air gets between the two backings. The carpet loses its dimensional stability and must be replaced.

Most primary backings are made in two shades, light or dark, depending on the color of the yarns that are tufted into the backing. As noted earlier, when a carpet is installed over a stair nose or other similarly curved area, the fabric can separate along its rows and will expose the backing. This is called *grinning*. Even heavy fabrics grin under the right conditions. A colored backing blends in better with the face yarns and creates the appearance of a thicker carpet.

Yarns tufted into the primary backing are only loosely inserted. They must be strongly locked into the primary to withstand scuffing, pulling, and vacuuming. Once the face yarns are stitched in, the fabric moves under a roller that applies a thin, even coating of a liquid latex emulsion across the entire width. The latex acts as a glue and permanently binds the face yarns to the primary backing (Figure 1-9). The amount of latex that is applied is measured in ounces per square yard. The thicker the tufts and the tighter the gauge, the more latex is used.

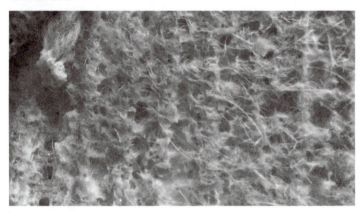

**Figure 1-9. Latexed primary backing.**

At this point in the manufacturing process, mills have an option. They can take various steps to finish the carpet, including dyeing, applying stain protection, and final shearing, or they can add a *secondary backing* and then finish the carpet. Virtually all residential carpet comes with a secondary backing that is used to cover the exposed latex rows (Figures 1-10 and 1-11). It makes a stiffer, heavier fabric—one with more "hand" and dimensional stability. The secondary backing also helps when installing the carpet.

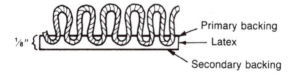

**Figure 1-10. Side view of tufted pile carpet. The secondary backing covers the rows of yarn.**

Like the primary backing, secondary backings are made from olefin. The secondary backing is what you see when the carpet is turned over. Secondary backings are woven using a combination of slit film and spun olefin. The slit film is the same flat thread used in the primary backings and runs widthwise. The spun olefin looks like round thread and runs lengthwise. The quality of the backing is determined by the *pic count*. This is the number of spun olefin yarns in one inch. A pic count ranges from 5 (wide apart) to 11 (closely spaced) spun yarns per inch. The difference is very noticeable when you turn carpet samples over and compare different secondary backings.

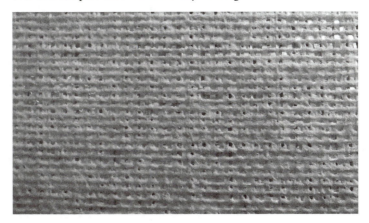

**Figure 1-11. Secondary backing.**

**SECRET:** People will tell you that the pic count is not important. It isn't important in order to get a good installation. (More about this later.) But it is one way for a manufacturer to have a built-in cost savings without having the exposed part of the carpet (fuzzy side up!) looking cheap. A heavier secondary backing also provides additional cushion for the face yarns, helping to prolong the life of the carpet.

The secondary backing is latexed and applied to the primary backing using rollers similar to those that fed the primary backing to the tufting needles earlier in the process. The two backings are firmly pressed together. Then the fabric passes through an oven that cures the latex.

The yarns, latex, and backings are fused into a strong floor covering.

The tufting machines combine face yarns, primary backings, latex, and secondary backings rapidly. High speed tufters easily produce several hundred square yards of carpet in a day. Rapid production means lower prices. Tufted carpet is less expensive than woven fabrics because it takes much longer to make woven carpet. Also, tufted carpet is usually made using less expensive synthetic fibers. Woven carpets are generally made from wool or wool-blend fibers, which are much more costly. The combination of large volume and less costly materials makes a less expensive carpet that still delivers a good value. Tufted carpet is also made in a wider variety of styles, patterns, and colors than woven carpets.

Whether you choose woven or tufted carpet, the choice is so wide that you are bound to find something to meet your needs—beautiful colors, long wear, and increased value for your home.

# 2

# CARPET YARNS

When people shop for carpet, one of the first questions they ask about any style is, "What's it made of?" The selection of the right face yarn, or pile fiber, is the most important factor affecting the wear and performance of the carpet. Conflicting ads and claims are confusing. Each one promises the "best" carpet fiber. The different fibers each offer advantages and disadvantages to you. You must decide which one best meets *your* needs.

To help you with your selection, carpet manufacturers have developed performance ratings for their carpets. When you turn a carpet sample over, you'll probably see a label that indicates the relative performance of that particular fabric. The ratings are based on a combination of face weight, twist level, and density. The ratings are usually numbered 1–5. Five is the highest rating, with perfect performance under heavy wear. One is the lowest. You'll probably never see a 1 or a 5. A rating over 4 means that the carpet should hold up well in your home under heavy traffic. A rating of 2.5–4 means the carpet should look good under "normal" use. Less than 2.5 means the fabric is built for light use. Keep in mind the term "relative." Because carpet life is determined by traffic (family size), home size, cleaning, etc., these ratings are meant as a guide only. Do not buy a carpet strictly because of its performance rating. You could be disappointed with your selection.

## NATURAL FIBERS (WOOL)

Wool is the original green, environmentally sustainable fiber. It is made from the shorn hair of sheep and has been used as a floor covering for at least 4,000 years! Wool is the most widely used natural fiber for pile yarns, and only a certain kind of wool is suitable for carpeting. Some sheep breeds produce excellent soft wool for clothing. But it is not resilient enough for floor coverings. Breeders use special sheep to produce the tough wool that goes into carpeting. The largest producers of this special carpet wool are found in Great Britain, Australia, and New Zealand.

Such a restricted supply cannot come close to meeting the world's demand for this luxurious resource. As a result, wool is the benchmark by which synthetic yarns are measured. It is the most expensive of all pile yarns used in wall to wall carpeting and is found in higher priced carpets. Yet even with its higher price, good quality wool broadloom is economical because it lasts so long. It is common to see 20-year-old carpet still giving good service. In all, wool accounts for about 3 percent of total carpet production, residential and commercial.

## Advantages of Wool

*Why does wool make such a good carpet?* First, it is very soft yet very resilient. When walked on, it springs back to its original appearance. Furniture marks easily brush or vacuum out. Under a microscope, a wool filament has a fish-scale look. This rough surface hides dirt, making the carpet look cleaner. The filaments also diffuse light that strikes the fabric, softening the color and overall appearance. Wool wears well, but must be made in a heavier fabric than synthetics to hold up under heavy use.

Much of today's wool carpeting is a blend of 80 percent wool and 20 percent nylon. You can find 80 percent wool, 10 percent nylon, and 10 percent polyester blends as well. The nylon adds "wearability" and helps lower the price somewhat. The blends with polyester use a special meltbond process. The blended yarn is subjected to low heat that fuses the polyester to adjacent fibers, creating a web-like structure. This "web" helps minimize shedding and improves the long term appearance of the carpet.

Another reason wool makes excellent carpet is that it dyes easily. Wool absorbs a lot of moisture, 15 to 18 percent. Wool also has a high protein content with naturally occurring dye sites. This combination allows for depth of shade and clarity of color. In addition, the sheep bred and raised to grow wool for carpet produce a fiber that is exceptionally white. This whiteness allows the dyeing of wool yarns in very light and very dark colors. In addition, the dyes are drawn into the molecular structure of the fiber, so the color is locked in. Wool fiber is color fast. Soil and dirt clean out easily.

Wool is permanently mothproofed by the manufacturers. It can also be treated for static electricity in low-humidity climates.

## Disadvantages of Wool

*So what's not to like?* The biggest drawback is staining. Because it absorbs so much moisture, it naturally absorbs contaminants from spills. Fluorochemical-based anti-soil agents, like Scotchgard®, help repel spills. But common spills like red wine or Kool-Aid®, which don't affect stain resist nylon fiber, will stain wool.

The other disadvantage is cost. Wool is a premium product. There's no way around that. Many carpet stores don't even have wool samples on the showroom floor because many people are cost conscious. If you have a limited budget, don't look for wool carpet.

## Processing Wool

The story of changing from animal hair into beautiful carpet for your home is a fascinating one. Each year great herds of different sheep breeds are shorn of their wool. Each breed grows wool with different characteristics. Some have a longer fleece (staple length), some produce a bulky wool, others grow a lustrous fleece. The raw wool is graded and shipped to a processor.

These different wools are blended together to make a combination of characteristics that the carpet designer wants in the finished carpet. Since sheep range wild, their fleece collects seeds, twigs, and dirt. The wool is cleaned, untangled, and carded (combed).

## Spinning the Wool

Two main methods, or systems, are used for spinning wool fibers into wool yarn for carpeting: *worsted* and *woolen*.

The worsted spinning system uses relatively long staple fibers in the 5- to 8-inch range. The fibers are blended, carded and combed (combed with progressively finer wires). A *sliver* (pronounced *SLY-ver*), or untwisted rope, is formed. Then the shortest fibers are combed out. The result is a parallel, untwisted strand of yarn. When the yarn is elongated and twist is applied, the compact finished yarn has a smooth, hard, lustrous surface. Worsted yarns are generally used for fine-gauge tufted carpet and for woven Wiltons.

Woolen spinning uses shorter (3½ to 5½ inches), more highly crimped staple fibers. The woolen carding system overlays or crosses the fibers, rather than combing them into uniform parallel slivers. This loose assembly of staple fibers is called a *roving*. It is twisted directly into a yarn characterized by a soft, loose, and bulky appearance. The woolen system allows wool with different characteristics to be blended while maintaining yarn evenness. Woolen spun yarns are well suited for carpeting because of their bulk and resilience. They are used in tufted and woven carpets.

## Dyeing the Wool

Once the fibers are spun into the desired yarn, the yarn is wound and prepared for dyeing. Two methods are generally used: *skein* dyeing and *piece* dyeing.

Skein dyeing places many skeins, or bundles, in the dye vat at one time. It takes a lot of yarn to make one roll of carpet, and many rolls must be made from the same *dye lot*, or dye run. Large installations use multiple rolls of carpet, and each roll must be virtually the same color so that when laid side by side there are no color variations. After dyeing, the skeins of yarn are wound onto large cones or spools. The yarn is now ready to be tufted or woven into a floor covering to grace your home.

One can also tuft undyed yarn into a carpet first and then dye the fabric in a large vat. This is known as *piece dyeing*. The dye vats are so large that several rolls of carpet are placed in them at one time. The rolls are tumbled in the hot dye bath for several hours to ensure even coloring and a large dye lot.

## SYNTHETIC FIBERS

When you go into a store to begin your search for the perfect carpet, most of the carpet samples you'll see are made from synthetic fibers. Three different oil-based manmade fibers are used in carpets today. The most popular is nylon, followed by polyester and olefin. Nylon and polyester fibers are also used in clothing. But the molecular structure of the filaments used in carpeting is different because carpets have different characteristics than clothing. Some of these characteristics are long wear and stain resistance.

## Nylon

Nylon is the most popular carpet fiber. It accounts for around 65 percent of carpet production. Nylon was developed in the late 1930s and was marketed most successfully in the '50s and '60s under Du-Pont's trademark "501" nylon. Today, Stainmaster® is probably the most recognized nylon brand.

With nylon, the floor-covering industry has a steady supply of a relatively low-priced fiber, compared to wool. Nylon also wears better than wool, given equal face weights. Nylon is easier to dye to a precise color because raw nylon has no color; it is completely clear.

Nylon is made from a petroleum derivative. Solid chips are melted and blended with a liquid formula. The solution is forced through a showerhead-like device with tiny, shaped holes, called a *spinnerette.* The shape and denier of the filament is determined by the shape and diameter of the spinnerette holes. Each nylon brand uses a differently shaped fiber (Figures 2-1 and 2-2). The trend is toward finer denier (soft feel) filaments. As the filaments are exposed to air, they harden into a continuous strand. The filaments are then wound for further processing. Nylon is made in both *BCF* (bulked continuous filament) and *staple fibers.*

**Figure 2-1. Hollow nylon fibers.**

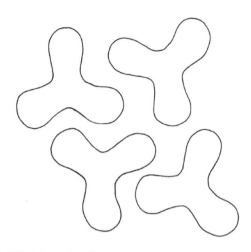

**Figure 2-2. Trilobular nylon fibers.**

**BCF Nylon.** Before being spun into yarn, the filaments are texturized by either a mechanical or a chemical process. They go from straight fibers to ones that have curls or crimps. This means that they have more bulk (more air between the filaments) and can cover more surface area than untexturized fibers. It also means that once the filaments are spun into yarn bundles, the finished carpet yarn has more resiliency and springs back to its original shape more easily.

When the BCF fibers are spun, they are twisted together to form a single ply yarn. A *ply* refers to one spun yarn bundle or one strand. The thickness of the ply depends on the number of filaments twisted together and the denier of the filaments. The diameter of the ply affects the finished texture of the carpet. Carpet yarns are either two or three ply. Plied yarns are also called cords. Once the filaments are twisted and plied, the yarn is wound and heat-set.

*Heat-setting* is a process similar to a permanent-wave treatment for your hair. It gives the yarn a "memory." The plied yarns are subjected to heat, pressure, and/or steam (depending on the method used) for a predetermined time. After heat-setting, the yarns keep their twist and resilience, even with a lot of use and repeated cleanings. In fact, hot-water extraction actually helps reset the twist and restore the carpet's appearance.

The industry trend is moving towards BCF with a finer denier. This makes a softer carpet with a cleaner look.

**Staple Yarn.** Continuous filament fibers are used to make staple yarn. BCF is cut into short filaments. The lengths range from 3 to 8 inches, depending on the desired look and texture of the finished carpet. After a series of combing and blending operations, the staple fiber is ready for spinning into yarn. The process is similar to the one described earlier for spinning wool. Both the woolen and worsted systems are used.

Staple yarns are popular with carpet mills, making up two-thirds of the production at some mills. Although extra steps are needed to make the yarn, it has advantages over BCF. Staple yarns, regardless of fiber type, offer greater coverage than BCF for a given face yarn weight. This means that staple face yarns appear thicker and heavier than BCF. To put this another way, more BCF yarn is needed to make a carpet look as thick as if it were made from staple yarn.

However, staple yarn is by nature a fuzzier yarn than BCF. Staple fabrics shed at least a little throughout their lifespan. They cannot achieve the same clean finish as BCF. Some carpet textures look better using staple yarn than BCF, however. It all depends on what you are looking for. BCF's lack of shed or lint makes the carpet easier to maintain. Staple fabrics can cost less than BCF because less staple yarn is used to make the carpet look as heavy.

Staple and BCF yarns are both very tough. Nylon has excellent abrasion resistance. Just walking on a nylon carpet will never wear it out, even with a lot of traffic. A carpet wears or gets thin because the yarn physically abrades away. This happens when the fabric is allowed to get dirty and remain soiled so that grit and sand actually cut away fiber. The cut fibers are vacuumed up and the carpet pile slowly disappears. This is why regular maintenance is so important to the life of a carpet.

Nylon cleans as easily as wool but dries more quickly. Nylon absorbs less moisture than wool—1 percent for nylon versus 17 percent for wool.

In addition, nylon does not support mold or mildew so it is non-allergenic. All nylon is engineered to eliminate static electricity in all but the driest climates.

What really established nylon as the fiber of choice was the introduction of "stain blocking" nylon carpet fiber in the late 1980s. Nylon was always plagued by relatively easy staining. Before then, if you spilled red wine or grape juice on a nylon carpet, you were sure to have a stained carpet even if you cleaned up the spill immediately. Nylon fiber has dye sites along its length. Think of the fiber as a plastic sponge with tiny holes all over it. These holes allow the fiber to accept dye and hold the color. Carpets are dyed using "acid" dyes. Most foods are acid based. Unfortunately, the dye sites are not completely filled or closed after dyeing. So when you spill something onto the carpet, the dye sites accept the spill as if it is dye. You wind up with a permanent stain. The stain-blocking chemistry closes the dye sites after dyeing and practically eliminates staining from food and drink spills. Stain-resist treated nylon carpet is not stain-proof, however.

Each brand of stain-resist carpet fiber has certain exclusions in its warranties. These might include non-food and beverage stains caused by cosmetics, bleaches, or inks; stains caused by substances that destroy or change the color of the carpet by dyes (such as food coloring or clothing), acne medicines (they slowly bleach), drain cleaners, and plant food; and human or other pet stains (such as vomit, blood, or feces). Even with these exclusions, an active family and carpeting get along well these days.

Stainmaster® nylon fiber was originally developed by Du-Pont and was the first heavily marketed brand of nylon with stain resistant qualities. Today, Stainmaster® nylon fiber is sold by Invista to many mills. Shaw Industries markets Anso brand stain-resist nylon, and Mohawk markets the Wear-Dated® of stain-resist nylon.

Besides these brand names, the industry also sells unbranded or generic nylon fiber. Unbranded and generic nylons cost less.

**SECRET:** The branded nylons are sometimes marketed under a mill's fiber name or as unbranded nylon. These nylon fibers have exactly the same stain-blocking levels as the brand names. But you'll have to ask your retailer to tell you this information. You will have no way to figure it out on your own. The unbranded and generics have a more limited warranty regarding stains, wear, and texture retention than the branded nylons. But an unbranded nylon carpet could be just right for you and will save you money.

Nylon fiber has also "gone green." Many recycling centers around the country accept used carpeting. The nylon face fibers are removed, sent to a processing center, and remelted into new nylon polymers.

Originally, nylon was known as a coarse fiber. The newest generations of nylon are soft. Marketed under many brands, these fine-denier nylons perform as well as the older, coarser nylons but are luxurious to the touch. The finest denier nylon carpets feel almost as soft as silk, but with excellent stain, wear, and texture-retention features.

## Polyester

Oil-derived polyester fibers were first used in carpeting around 1960. Polyester was lower priced than nylon. The early polyesters featured gorgeous colors but were shiny and did not hold up under a lot of use. Some of the first polyester carpets were made with "singles" yarns, not a two-ply yarn. These "singles" had no resiliency and flattened down quickly. When plied yarns were used in carpeting, the yarns were not sufficiently heat set. They untwisted rapidly and the carpet matted badly. Polyester carpeting got a bad reputation, which it is still fighting today.

Polyester has its advantages. It costs less than nylon. When it is solution dyed, it is practically fade proof. It is also made white, ready to dye. Its color palette is wide. Properly engineered polyester carpet gives a lot of value for the price. It is made as a staple and as BCF. Polyester also has a soft hand to compete with the soft-touch nylons.

And it is a recycled product. Virtually all polyester carpet fiber, called PET (polyethylene terephthalate), is made from recycled soda and water bottles. Mohawk Flooring and Shaw Industries are leaders in recycling these bottles into carpet fiber. In fact, Mohawk states that one in four recycled plastic bottles—over 3 billion a year in the United States—is turned into its branded polyester carpet.

Polyester naturally resists staining. It offers excellent stain resistance to water-based spills and good resistance to oil-based spills. Overall, it cleans well when a hot-water extraction system is used.

To compete with nylon, polyester carpets are sold with strong prorated and non-prorated warranties covering stains, wear, and texture retention. Most polyester carpets are made in heavier weights than nylon, and for a comparable or lower price. You might be surprised when you look at carpet samples made from polyester. You'll see a lot of carpet for the money.

In 2004, a variant of carpet polyester came on the market. It was originally developed by Shell Oil and DuPont in the 1980s. The Federal Trade Commission recognized it as a distinct fiber, called *triexta*, or *PTT*, in 2009. Today it is sold under the Smartstrand® brand by Mohawk.

DuPont uses a patented process that includes fermented corn sugar as an ingredient to make a renewably sourced polymer they call *Sorona®*. Corn sugar comprises 37 percent of Sorona®. Then Mohawk spins the Sorona® polymer into their Smartstrand® fiber and tufts it into carpeting. The fiber has excellent stain resistance because of a built-in, not applied, stain-block treatment.

Mohawk is very proud of its exclusive carpet fiber, stating that it has superior resistance to stains, soil, pet urine, static, fading, and abrasion, with outstanding texture retention. Mohawk has given carpet made with this fiber one of the best non-prorated warranties in the industry. That is certainly a sign of confidence on their part.

The newest polyester fiber comes from Stainmaster® (Invista). The company realized it was missing some business because Stainmaster® nylon is more expensive than any polyester. So to meet a price point, the company developed Essentials® polyester. It is made by select mills only and sold through select retailers. Invista has given it a strong warranty to match the Stainmaster® name.

Polyester carpet fiber has one main drawback when compared to nylon: a lower resistance to abrasion. Abrasion is the ability of a fiber to withstand *wear*, which is defined as traffic-related reduction in pile density. Polyester fiber is softer than nylon. Here, "soft" does not mean how it feels when you touch the fiber. Just as glass is softer than diamond (diamond cuts glass), it means that polyester does not stand up to abrasion as well as does nylon fiber. Keep in mind, though, that this is a relative statement: The heavier construction weights used to make polyester carpets negate the lower abrasion resistance of polyester. That is why manufacturers can give their polyester carpets a great wear warranty.

## Olefin (Polypropylene)

Olefin, also called polypropylene, is another type of fiber used in carpeting. Most primary and secondary backings used in tufted carpet are made from olefin. It is also used in carpet face pile, including outdoor carpet and synthetic turf.

Olefin is an oil-based fiber made from polymer chips that are melted and then extruded into continuous filaments. It was first used in carpeting in the 1970s and gained widespread acceptance in the 1980s.

Olefin does not absorb water. It is the only synthetic carpet fiber that floats. Olefin must be solution dyed—in its liquid form—

before extrusion. This process makes the dye part of the molecular structure of the fiber and gives olefin outstanding fade and stain resistance. When ultraviolet blockers are included in the dyestuffs, the outdoor olefin carpet will not sun fade. Because it resists water, it is extremely difficult for water-based spills to stain it. Oil-based spills are harder to remove. You can spot-clean olefin carpet with chlorine bleach, and you will not harm the color. For overall cleaning, the hot-water extraction method is best. Olefin is a strong fiber; it resists abrasion and wears well when made using appropriate constructions. It is also moisture and mildew resistant.

Olefin is not a resilient fiber, however; it tends to flatten down under high traffic. That is why you will see olefin made in tight level-loop designs or heavy Berber style fabrics. Olefin has a low melting point. High friction—for example, generated from the wheels of a toy racecar—will melt the fiber.

You must decide which fiber works best in your home. Each has pros and cons. There is no one "best" carpet fiber. The combinations of fiber, color, style, and price will help you make the right choice.

# 3

# CARPET STYLES & TEXTURES

Any of the carpet fibers can be made into a wide variety of textures and patterns (Figure 3-1). Each connotes a certain lifestyle, ranging from casual to formal elegance. You decide which "look" works best in your home. Styles and textures, like colors, change over the years. Long shags were popular many years ago. Then they lost their appeal. Now shorter shags are in style.

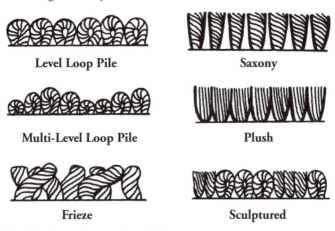

**Level Loop Pile**

**Saxony**

**Multi-Level Loop Pile**

**Plush**

**Frieze**

**Sculptured**

**Figure 3-1. Carpet fibers: styles and textures.**

Texture is made in many ways. Tufted carpet normally produces a flat, level-loop texture. By changing the tension of the yarn and the depth of needle penetration, patterns—high and low loops—are created. When the loop is cut, the carpet becomes a cut-pile.

Varying the tuft thickness (number of plies) and tuft length makes other looks. Yarns that are tightly or loosely twisted change the look again. Changing the density also changes the look.

Combining cut and uncut pile produces different textures. By combining various combinations, entirely new textures are made. Adding creative colorations further changes the apparent textures. One or another of these variations is always in style. Improvements in weaving and tufting techniques have also produced carpet with many more textures.

With so many different texture combinations (14 textures plus "other" are listed on my carpet inspection report form, for example), it is necessary to divide them into two primary groups: *loop-pile* and *cut-pile* fabrics. The loop-piles include *level loop, high-low loop, patterned loop,* and *tip-shear.* The cut-pile group includes *cut-pile,* (plush or velvet), *cut and loop, multilevel cut pile, patterned cut pile, cut Berber, Saxony, textured Saxony,* and *frieze* (pronounced *free-ZAY*).

## LOOP PILE

*Level loop* describes the weaving or tufting of face yarns into a carpet that appears flat and is made of rows of looped face yarns all the same height. It is the best wearing of all textures because more of the face yarns are exposed to the surface. It also keeps its original appearance better than any other style. The shorter the pile and the closer the rows, the better wearing the carpet. Level loop is widely used in commercial installations. Residentially, it is good for stairways, hallways, family/great rooms, or anywhere else a carpet will get hard use. It also is easy to spot clean. Wool, nylon, polyester, and olefin fibers are usually used in this type of construction. Berber is one style that uses level loop-pile (Figure 3-2).

*High-low loop* carpets are made by both tufting or weaving (Figure 3-3). The texture is created by making some loops high and some loops low. Alternating high/low rows makes a corrugated or corduroy effect (Figure 3-4). Random high-low loops make a carpet with a nubby, casual appearance. This texture, like level loop, wears extremely well. Wool, nylon, polyester, and olefin are usually the fibers of choice. High-low loop carpet has a tendency to crush slightly more than level-loop because of the longer loops. The longer the fabric, the more it will crush with use, whether or not it is looped. High-low loop is a good style for high-use rooms such as family or rec rooms, home offices, hallways, and stairs—wherever a casual look is needed.

*Scrolled* or *carved* carpet is a patterned high-low loop variation (Figure 3-5). This classic style is always popular with homeowners, especially those wanting a more formal look. A pattern, usually a leaf or its variation, is made by high and low loops and appears carved into the face of the pile. The depth of the pattern depends on the thickness of the material. The design originated with hand-carved Oriental rugs. Carved patterns also wear well.

**Figure 3-2. Berber (wool).**

**Figure 3-3. High-low loop.**

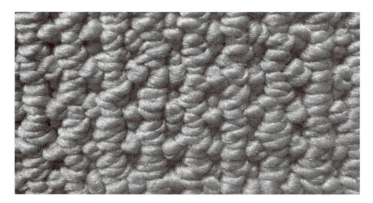

Figure 3-4. Corduroy.

Figure 3-5. High-low loop variation

Figure 3-6. Tip shear.

*Tip-sheared* fabrics (Figure 3-6) are used in both residential and commercial applications. They are made by cutting and shearing some loops while leaving others looped. Tip-shearing creates different patterns, such as variegated loop, alternating with rows of cut and uncut pile, or random shearing, which gives a dappled effect. Tip-shearing combines the best of plush and loop piles. The evenness of the plush is broken up by the rugged texture of the loops. Tip shear combines a casual and formal look. The cut portions are smooth and elegant, while the loops hide footprints and shading.

## CUT PILE

Cut pile is the second main texture group. It refers to any style fabric that is made from cut instead of looped face yarns. Wool and nylon are the two main fibers used to make cut-pile carpets, although you might find olefin or polyester cut-pile carpets.

*Velvet plush* and *Saxony plush* are both smooth, heavy, velvety piles of cut face yarns that are all the same height. A *velvet plush* fabric (Figure 3-7) is made of singles (unplied) or two-ply yarn tufted or woven so tightly that the yarns support each other and stand up. The yarn ends seem to blend together when sheared smooth. Many hand-made Oriental rugs are a singles plush. This texture is the most formal of all. (Velvet also refers to a particular method for weaving cut-pile fabrics.)

**Figure 3-7. Plush.**

*Saxony plushes* (Figure 3-8) are usually made from tightly twisted two-ply yarns. They tend to have a longer pile height than velvet plushes.

Because of the plied yarns and longer pile height, Saxony plushes do not have as smooth a finish as a velvet plush, but the overall look is still elegant and formal. They are called a *textured* or *pencil-point plush* when you can see the individual yarn ends. Textured plushes are also called "trackless" plushes because footprints and vacuum marks are less noticeable.

Plush fabrics must be made in relatively heavy weights (compared to loop piles) to wear well and maintain their original appearance. When compared to loop fabrics, plush fabrics also show footprints and vacuum marks and generally need more maintenance.

*Cut-and-loop* fabrics have some yarns cut and others looped (Figure 3-9). These designs are generally more casual. The pattern can be one height only, or it can be high and low, creating a cobblestone effect (Figure 3-10), flowers, or swirls (Figure 3-11). The pattern is also varied by using a Saxony plush or shag instead of plush in the cut-pile area of the design. Cut-and-loop probably provides the widest design variations of all the styles. Multi-level cut and loops create additional patterns or a random effect. This style hides dirt and stains since it usually comes in multicolor tones. It is also easy to maintain because it does not show footprints or traffic patterns as much as a plush.

*Shag* is the longest cut-pile style. (Figure 3-12). The style originated in California years ago. It is good for an easy-going, open lifestyle. It started as a 2-inch-long, floppy fabric, long enough to lose a cookie! It has evolved into shorter, denser fabrics that are easier to maintain. The government defines shag as any style longer than ¾ inch, but shag is generally longer than 1 inch.

*Frieze* is another classic style. It has been popular for decades. Although it appears to be a textured plush, it is actually made of thin, tightly twisted, heat-set yarns. It is tufted or woven into a cut-pile that is low, dense, and characterized by the twisted, kinky nature of the face yarns (Figure 3-13). Friezes are known for their excellent wearability. They lend an informal air to any room, and they hide traffic patterns and footprints. Nylon is most often used for frieze carpets.

A variation of the frieze is sometimes called a *cut Berber*. This face pile has thicker tufts than a classic frieze. The thicker tufts make a deeper pile with a nubbier texture. It is very popular in high-traffic areas like hallways and family rooms. As is true of frieze, nylon is the most popular fiber for a cut Berber.

Figure 3-8. Saxony plush.

Figure 3-9. Patterned cut and loop.

Figure 3-10. Cobblestone cut and loop.

Figure 3-11. Flower pattern.

Figure 3-12. Shag.

Figure 3-13. Frieze.

## CARPET AND INTERIOR DESIGN

Now let's review the different styles and textures according to room use. The living room is usually the showcase of the home. It is the first room that guests see when they step into your home, so it must look attractive and comfortable. If your living room is more for looking than for living—if it is not used much—then you can use light colors and delicate fabrics. Consider plush or Saxony, maybe even a wool Berber in a pastel shade. If the living room has the TV in it, then it gets a lot of use. Somewhat darker colors or a subtle pattern might just be the right thing. A tip-shear might work well, or try a patterned loop that won't "walk out." A rougher texture will take the spills, and a heavier fabric will hold up in a busy room.

The dining room is often attached to the living room, so it becomes an extension of the living room. Whatever you use in the living room will work fine in the dining room. If the room is off by itself, you might consider a fine plush, especially if the active living room has a carpet with a more casual texture.

The family room, halls, and steps are the main traffic areas in any home. It makes sense to put the sturdiest carpet and pad in these areas. The investment is well worth it. A heavy frieze, tightly twisted short cut-pile, or Berber will hold up under a lot of traffic. And remember, when a carpet is laid over the edge of a stair tread, the fabric has tendency to "grin," or separate along the rows of yarn and show the backing. Grinning can be avoided by using a carpet with a dense pile.

The bedrooms are good rooms in which to economize. They normally receive little use because they are empty most of the day. Putting a dense pad under a lighter-weight carpet is an easy way to give a luxury feel to a less expensive carpet. A better pad also makes the carpet wear better.

Lighter colors work well in a master bedroom, making the room look larger and more relaxing. Any texture works well, depending on your taste and decor. Try plush or Saxony, or maybe a cut and loop for variety. Subtle patterns or colorful pastels are fun in a girl's room, whereas a boy's room usually needs somewhat darker colors or prints. A sturdier fiber, like nylon, gives excellent service. Consider cut and loop or tip-sheared styles.

What about the bathroom? Many new homes come with a carpeted bath as an extension of the master bedroom. If you decide to put wall-to-wall carpet in a bathroom, it must be sturdy. This confined area gets direct water and high humidity. Make sure any cut-pile style used has a low pile and a tight twist. A low pile helps prevent crushing and matting in front of sinks and vanities.

# 4

# COLORS THAT DAZZLE

To most people, color is the most important consideration when buying carpet. The color not only adds beauty to the home, it ties together the rest of the furnishings. The carpet mills put a lot of time and effort into their color lines so that people will have a huge array of colors to choose from. The right colors in a new line can make it instantly popular.

## CREATING NEW COLORS AND STYLES

The creation of new patterns and colors is a slow and careful process. Generally, the larger mills have in-house artists. They are up on the latest trends and styles in the world of fashion. They often work closely with other fabric designers in the home furnishing industry, such as upholstery and drapery designers, to speculate on color trends two or three years from now. The Color Association of the United States (CAUS) is a color forecasting group. There is an "Interiors-Environmental" subgroup that works on color forecasting for the home. Many mill artists belong to this association.

The artists sometimes hand draw and paint new patterns, but they mostly use computers to design their new patterns. Different color combinations are created. Committees choose what they hope will be popular colorations and textures. Then the equipment is set up to produce trial runs in order to see if the finished product looks as good as the artist's rendition.

Just because something looks good on paper does not mean the actual fabric is something a shopper will want to buy. In fact, many "mill trials" never make it to the showroom.

Design and style are two costs that help determine the final price of a carpet line. High fashion and a wide range of colors are found only in the higher priced lines. Whatever is "hot" will cost more. Smaller mills usually do not have their own textile artists. They sometimes resort to copying popular designs from other mills in order to stay competitively priced.

Do you still want a plain-Jane beige carpet, knowing all the work that goes into creating those exciting colors and styles?

## DYE METHODS

The carpet industry uses several methods to dye fabrics. The type of dye system used for a specific carpet depends on the "look" the designer wants for the finished fabric. Synthetic carpet fibers are sometimes dyed before the actual filaments are formed. Wool and synthetic fibers are also dyed before they are made into a carpet. Other methods dye these fibers after the carpet is made.

Synthetic fibers are often dyed before fiber extrusion. This method is called *solution dyeing* because the color is added to the fiber material when it is in a liquid state. The dye becomes part of the molecular structure of the yarn fiber before the solution goes through the spinneret and turns into a solid fiber. Nylon, polyester, and olefin fibers are solution dyed. This method results in extremely fade-resistant yarn. It is excellent for regions with high humidity. Solution-dyed yarns work well in rooms that receive a lot of direct sunlight. Solution-dyed yarns are also used in outdoor carpet like artificial turf.

Three methods are used to dye raw fiber before it is made into carpet. Both woven and tufted carpet utilize yarns dyed with either method. With *stock-dyeing,* staple carpet fibers are dyed in bulk before being spun into yarn. Large batches of fibers, up to 1,000 pounds, are placed in pressurized dye vats, where heated dye is circulated through the fibers. After washing and drying, several batches of fiber are then blended to ensure even color throughout the entire lot. Wool and staple nylon fibers are typically dyed this way. After the fibers are dyed and blended, they are put through the spinning process and formed into carpet yarns.

*Skein dyeing* also uses staple fibers, but the raw fiber has already been spun into singles yarns and wound into a coil or skein. The skeins are dyed in large pressurized vats. After washing and drying, the dyed singles are ready to ply into finished carpet yarn.

The third dye method is called *space dyeing*. This technique uses continuous filament fibers to produce carpets with a tweed effect. Two different systems are used to make this interesting "look." One way lays hundreds of strands of undyed yarn parallel to each other. A series of rollers print a different color on each section of yarn. After fixing the color, the yarns are washed, dried, and wound in preparation for tufting. With the second method, sheets of yarn are printed by rollers. Each roller puts color on each side of the fabric. When finished, the colors are set and the yarns are washed and dried after unraveling. They are ready for tufting or weaving into a random tweed pile. Nylon is the most common fiber used for space dyeing.

Two main techniques are used to dye tufted carpet after the yarns have been tufted into the primary backing. Today, the most common dye method is *continuous dyeing*. This is also the most economical way for mills to dye carpet in large volumes. After tufting, greige (pronounced *gray*) goods (undyed yarn and the primary backing) are fed continuously through large dye machines. These machines have a tube above and across the moving carpet fitted with evenly spaced spray heads that apply dye directly onto the carpet moving below it. After dyeing, the carpet moves directly into a large steam chamber where the dye is set. The spray heads must be carefully calibrated; otherwise, one side of the carpet could be dyed slightly lighter or darker than the other side. This color difference becomes a problem during installation. (See Chapter 9: Side Match.) Years ago, continuous dyeing made only a solid-colored carpet. Today mills use specialized dyes, called *differential* dyes, that produce up to three dye levels—light, medium, and dark—on one dye run.

*Piece or beck dyeing* is the other technique used to dye post-tufted carpet. Beck dyeing uses smaller runs of carpet and is especially good when a custom color is ordered. Up to 200 yards of carpet are placed in a large tank called a dye beck. The greige goods are rotated through the hot dye until the correct color depth is achieved. By using differential dyes or differential dyeing fibers, a carpet with up to three shades is made from one batch of dye.

## COLOR CONSIDERATIONS

Of course, all of this just explains how the carpet is dyed. The most important thing to most people is the color itself. What color will look best in one particular room or throughout your home? How should you choose the right color that will make the right statement?

You've probably seen all the latest colors in the home magazines and fashion publications, and you've tried to keep up with the latest color trends. But what about your own color preferences? After all, we're talking about *your* home, not some abstract picture in a magazine. And keep in mind that today's "hot" color will look dated in a few years.

It is important to begin your search with a certain color in mind, but remember to be flexible. Designers are always coming up with new colors, tints, and shades. You just may walk into a carpet shop and fall in love with a color you've never seen! When looking for a color, take a paint chip or upholstery sample along. Also, a color might look wonderful under the showroom lights, but might look dull or unattractive in your own home with different colored walls and lights.

But before you choose a color, you must first understand a few basic things about how colors are made. *Primary colors*—red, yellow, blue—are colors already broken down into their basic components. Combinations of these three colors will make an almost infinite number of other colors and shades. A *color family* is formed by mixing the primary colors. There is a red/yellow family, a yellow/blue family, and a blue/red family. (Red and yellow make orange, yellow and blue make green, and blue and red make purple.)

Black and white are not technically considered colors. Black is a mixture of all colors, and white is the absence of color. Tints are made by adding white, and shades are made by adding black. Black tones down bright colors without detracting from them. White works well to moderate lighter colors.

### Color schemes

Once you have chosen a particular color, you are ready to devise a color scheme. All color schemes are variations of the three basic ways to combine colors as described above. Remember: choosing a color scheme is a matter of taste. There is no absolute right or wrong way to do it.

The three basic types of color schemes used to integrate the colors in a room and pull the room together are monochromatic, analogous, and complementary.

*Monochromatic,* or one color, schemes use one basic color along with tints (light) and shades (dark) of the same color. Blue can be used as a basic color, with violet and plum as accents.

Two or more related colors make an *analogous* color scheme. For example, smoky brown and eggshell work well together. Or plum, violet, and rose are lovely combinations. Plum could be the overall color, with violet and rose as the accents.

A *complementary* color scheme uses contrasting colors to create a dramatic setting. One color serves as the dominant scheme. The other color becomes the accent. Plum with pale yellow is a good example.

## Designing Tips

Keep these ideas in mind when considering color combinations:

- Whenever possible, use the carpet and walls as the basis for your color scheme. They are the largest areas in a room. You should plan around them for a unified design.
- When using darker shades for the carpet, the walls can be a lighter shade of the carpet.
- When using a light carpet, darker walls work well.
- Light carpeting makes a small room look larger. Darker colors make a large room look smaller and more cozy.
- Draperies work well to coordinate a color scheme when their color relates to the carpet, either through the pattern or by working with solid colors.
- Bright, warm colors work well in dark, poorly lit rooms and make the rooms more appealing and cheerful. Sunny rooms look cooler by using darker, more subtle colors.
- A well-conceived color scheme sets the mood of a room. Bright colors are more informal; elegant, subtle colors make a room more formal and conservative.

Your designer will be happy to work with you in order to design the home of your dreams!

# 5

# CARPET PADDING

Padding is also called cushion or underlayment. Padding is an underlayment between the floor and the carpet. A firm and resilient underlayment acts as a shock absorber that prevents the carpet, when walked upon, from "bottoming out" and rubbing on the hard floor underneath. This friction contributes to carpet wear.

Even though proper padding is so important, it is often only an afterthought that buyers have when purchasing a carpet. Many retailers include the cost of carpet, pad and installation into one "sale" price. Like many other retail sales schemes, the items included in the package are "low end" to make the price seem attractive and to get you in the door. Salespeople will definitely try to upgrade you to better quality carpet and pad. Remember that by putting a little extra into a better pad, you can extend—sometimes by 50 percent—the life of the carpet. On better quality cushion, many manufacturers will replace the underlayment if it ever flattens out during the life of the installation.

If a pad is too thick or too soft, the carpet flexes too much. This type of movement will cause a properly installed carpet to loosen and wrinkle over time. It can also make seams come apart and the carpet backing separate (delaminate). For these reasons, the carpet industry has minimum standards for all pads. Generally, for residential installations, the pad should have a minimum density of six pounds and a maximum thickness of $7/16$ inch. For Berber and low-profile styles, an eight-pound density and $3/8$ inch thickness is recommended. Remember, thicker and softer are not necessarily better.

# TYPES OF PADDING

With all the choices available, selecting the right carpet pad can be confusing. For this reason, a closer look at various types of cushion will help you with your choice.

## Fiber Pads

The oldest type of underlayment is made from natural fibers. It is called the *hair and jute* pad, or combination pad. This pad looks like thick felt and is made from a combination of pressed animal hair, usually cow or horse, and jute or recycled fibers. Jute is a vegetable fiber. A combination pad provides the firmest *step,* or feel underfoot, of all the pads. It is sold by weight or thickness. Weight ranges from 32 ounces to around 80 ounces per square yard. Thickness ranges from ¼ to ½ inch. It is particularly recommended under any type of woven carpet. It allows woven or tufted carpet to maintain its tight stretch because the firm felt underlayment allows very little "give." If you use a walker, wheelchair, or electric scooter, a fiber pad withstands the pressure from the wheels and the rolling movement better than other pads.

Synthetic fiber cushion (Figure 5-1), made from nylon, polyester, or polypropylene (olefin), has one inherent advantage over natural fiber cushion: It withstands moisture and will not support mildew growth. You might consider synthetic fiber underlayment if you live in a damp or flood-prone area.

Figure 5-1. Synthetic fiber pad. (Photo courtesy of Leggett & Platt)

Fiber pads are usually rubberized on one side to provide good adherence to the subfloor. The smooth side faces up to allow the carpet to slide over it during installation.

Both types of fiber pad are rated for light, medium, or heavy use. They are among the higher priced underlayments.

## Foam Pads

Foam, or technically polyurethane foam, pads make up the largest percentage by sales of carpet cushion. The three types of foam pads are measured by density, which is weight divided by thickness. They are measured in pounds per cubic foot. The various cushions are also sold in different thicknesses.

The most commonly used pad is *rebond*, also called bonded or bonded polyurethane pad (Figure 5-2). Rebond accounts for up to 85 percent of all cushion sales. You will easily spot it on the sample racks. Rebond is the only speckled, multicolored pad you'll see. It is a true green product made from new and post-consumer scrap. It is made from recycled scrap foam and sponge rubber swept off the production lines of furniture makers and other foam users. Used pad of all types is also recycled into new rebond pad. The pieces are chopped into a uniform size and pressed together under pressure into huge "cakes." The amount of pressure determines the density of the finished product. The cakes are then sliced into the desired thickness. A net or plastic sheet is added to the top side of the pad, which helps hold the pad together. It also allows the carpet to slide over the pad during installation. The sheets are then rolled and wrapped.

**Figure 5-2. Rebond (bonded) pad. (Photo courtesy of Leggett & Platt)**

Rebond comes in several thicknesses (from ⅜ to ½ inch) and densities (from 5 to 10 pounds per cubic foot), depending on the type of carpet and the way you want the pad to feel under the carpet. The main objection to rebond pad is the perceived lack of uniformity because of the variation in materials. In fact, given the proper density and thickness of the cushion for the type of installation, it holds up under any type of traffic. This is why it is the most popular type of pad. It ranges in price from low to medium-high.

*Prime polyurethane foam* cushion (Figure 5-3), also called densified urethane or prime urethane, is made by combining liquid ingredients in a block form. This is the same type of foam used in furniture and automobile seats. The density of the finished foam is determined by the proportions of the chemicals and the cell size. Once the foam has cured, it is sliced into sheets. The sheets are glued together into rolls. Carpet cushion foam is much more dense than furniture foam. Prime foam is sold by density and thickness. In an effort to be "green," some prime foams are made using soy, vegetable, or sunflower oil as part of the liquid ingredients. Some carpet manufacturers will double their texture-retention warranty when an approved prime urethane pad is used under their carpet.

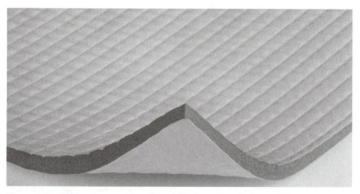

**Figure 5-3. Prime polyurethane (densified urethane) foam pad. (Photo courtesy of Legget & Platt)**

*Froth polyurethane foam* is made with carpet backing machinery. Liquid ingredients are applied, either directly to the backs of some carpet styles, or to a non-woven material (for making separate cushion). They react and form a thin, dense foam that is particularly useful in commercial applications with wide expanses of carpet.

## Rubber Pads

Rubber pads fall into two groups. *Textured* or *waffle* pads are easily recognized. They have a bumpy appearance (Figure 5-4). Waffle pads are made by pouring aerated liquid rubber into molds, similar to a large waffle iron, to form sheets. After curing and cooling, a material is glued to the top to aid during the carpet installation. Then the sheets are joined and formed into rolls.

The best waffle pads are made with a high percentage of natural or synthetic rubber. Unfortunately, many are made with a lot of filler material that dries out and turns to powder in just a few years. You must depend on the retailer's integrity to help you choose a quality waffle pad.

Waffle pad is sold by weight, ranging from 32 to 100 ounces per square yard. The 100-ounce cushion gives what has been described as an "executive feel" underfoot.

Figure 5-4. Textured or waffle pad. (Photo courtesy of Leggett & Platt)

Its main drawback is that carpets can stretch severely after installation because of the extra flex from the bumps in the pad. It is best to choose a waffle pad that has a smaller "bump." Woven carpets should never be installed over a waffle pad, no matter what the configuration of the bumps or the weight of the pad. Carpets made with a non-woven primary or secondary backing should not be installed over a waffle pad, either. Instead, these types of carpet work best over a smooth, firm pad.

A *flat rubber* pad (Figure 5-5), also called slab rubber, is more firm and supportive than a waffle pad. Because it is firm, dense, and flat, a sponge-rubber cushion is perfect under a woven carpet. It also works well with Berbers and other low profile styles as well as carpets made with non-woven backings. It is made using cured natural or synthetic rubber and is formed into sheets. After a top sheet of synthetic material, which aids in carpet installation, is added, the sheets are joined and rolled. Flat rubber pads are sold by weight and thickness.

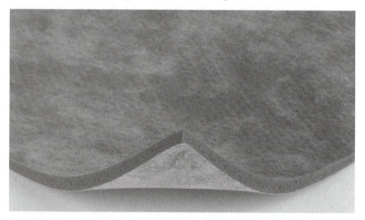

Figure 5-5. Flat or slab rubber pad. (Photo courtesy of Platt & Leggett)

## MORE BENEFITS OF PADDING

According to the Carpet Cushion Council, separate carpet cushion offers the following advantages to carpet installations:

- Carpet cushion can add a useful life to a carpet.
- A carpet installed over separate cushion can be more economical.
- Carpet cushion makes a carpet seem richer and more luxurious.
- Carpet cushion can significantly improve a carpet's acoustical properties.
- Carpet cushion can improve the thermal insulation properties of the floor covering.
- Carpet cushion can reduce the impact exerted on floor covering by one-half.
- Maintenance costs are often lower during a cushioned carpet's life.
- Carpets with separate cushion can be less costly to install.

**Carpet cushion can add a useful life to a carpet.** A common misconception made about cushion is that you can save money by increasing the pile weight of a carpet and eliminating the cushion. Actually, a cushion may result in more useful life in some carpet applications than slightly heavier unprotected carpet can offer.

Carpet is seldom replaced because it "wears" out. It is usually changed because it "uglies" out—or loses its fresh, new appearance. By reducing pile-height loss and pile crushing, cushion can help keep a carpet "new" looking—and therefore stretch its usable life span.

**A carpet installed over separate cushion can be more economical.** Separate cushion can prove to be the most economical installation over a period of time. In wear resistance tests done by Independent Textile Testing Service, a variety of cushion types added to the wear resistance of carpet.

And in a test to determine loss of pile height, which gives the appearance of wear, carpets without cushion showed a 19.3 percent loss in thickness. Carpets with cushion may suffer only 5 to 10 percent pile-height loss. So an installation with cushion can be more economical, since most carpets without any form of cushion may need to be replaced sooner. The fibers of a carpet installed without cushion can become compacted more easily, and the "new" look of the carpet may disappear more quickly.

**Carpet cushion makes a carpet seem richer and more luxurious.** The most universally accepted benefits of carpet cushion are that it makes a carpet feel better and look better longer.

While the luxury is a subjective quality and cannot be measured, cushion does impart resiliency and resistance to pressure, which contribute to a carpet's feeling of luxury.

In research conducted by Independent Textile Testing Service, a test was used whereby different carpet/cushion systems were subjected to rolling a chair with 150-pound weight over them 20,000 times. The results indicated that carpets with no cushion had an average of 19.3 percent loss in pile height (thickness) as opposed to a 5 to 10 percent loss in thickness for carpets with a separate cushion. The favorable effect of cushion in reducing the appearance of wear was indicated by decreased loss in thickness. So, since carpets with separate cushion remain thicker, they could also appear more luxurious for a longer period of time. And with separate cushion, it's possible to select the degree of luxury or firmness of tread you desire.

**Carpet cushion can significantly improve a carpet's acoustical properties.** A carpeted environment is quiet because the pile surface absorbs surface noise at the source. But a carpet installed with separate cushion can make the room even more quiet.

Tests conducted in the Kodaras Acoustical Laboratories reverberation chambers substantiate this. For example, in floor sound-absorption tests, a carpet laid directly on concrete floor, with no cushion, measured a Noise Reduction Coefficient of 0.25. In a like test, the same carpet with a cushion on a concrete floor measured a Noise Reduction Coefficient of 0.65, a considerably better performance.

Separate cushion can also reduce impact-noise transmission. On a concrete floor with no cushion, a carpet registered an impact noise rating of +14. The same carpet with separate cushion had an impact noise rating of +25—again, significant improvement.

**Carpet cushion can improve the thermal insulation properties of the floor covering.** Another of the undisputed qualities of carpet cushion is that it improves the overall thermal insulation properties of a floor covering.

In fact, typical carpet cushions have been measured to have "Rvalues" from 0.75 to 2.0. Rvalue is a way to measure a material's insulation efficiency. Carpet cushion helps reduce heat loss in a home.

**Carpet cushion can reduce the impact exerted on floor covering by one-half.** Another factor related to luxury is the underfoot cushioning properties imparted by carpet cushion.

In tests conducted at the University of Chicago, the effects of people's actually walking over carpet and cushion were measured. The tests revealed that carpet by itself and cushion by itself have only limited impact absorption value. However, when the carpet and carpet cushion are combined into a proper system, the ability of the floor covering to absorb walking impact rises dramatically. And this can improve your comfort by reducing walking fatigue.

**Maintenance costs are often lower during a cushioned carpet's life.** Vacuum cleaning is more efficient with separate cushion since most machines "lift" the carpet to provide air circulation, thus insuring maximum cleaning power. This can help reduce the grinding action of embedded dirt that can cut and fray fiber.

**Carpets with separate cushion can be less costly to install.** At first glance, carpet installations without separate cushion seem less costly. But upon further examination, it can be argued that they represent a false economy.

First, direct glue-down or attached cushion installation may be less expensive initially. But the difference could be made up in removing worn carpet in glue-down installation when labor costs for removal and clean up of the floor will most likely outweigh the original savings.

A carpet with separate carpet cushion will mask surface irregularities. A carpet alone cannot conceal crack and trowel marks as effectively as a carpet with cushion. This often means that less floor preparation is required before the carpet is installed.

In fact, a study of carpet workrooms (professional installers) indicated that when all installation factors are taken into consideration—floor preparation, carpet installation, carpet removal, and cleaning and repair of the floor after removal—the costs of a separate cushion are significantly reduced over that of a direct glue-down installation.

# 6

# BUYING CARPET

---

Now you are ready to begin your search for new carpet. Where do you look? How do you find a retailer? Like most things in life, you have many choices. This chapter will help you make the best decision.

In the "old" days (pre-1980), most people bought their carpet from a department store because that was where the manufacturers sold it. The carpet went from mill to distributor to department store. Specialty stores selling only carpeting were almost non-existent. Now, department stores don't sell floor coverings of any kind, except area rugs.

Today you can buy your carpet online, from a specialty floor covering retailer, from a "big box" home remodeling store, or through an interior designer.

**Buying online.** If you know how to properly measure your rooms, you know what you want to buy, and you have your own installer, then buying online can save you a lot of money. E-sellers don't have the same cost structure as brick and mortar stores. Rent, warehousing, shipping, advertising, utilities, employee payroll—all these expenses are greatly reduced or eliminated.

Several online sites sell carpet from the major mills, and they offer most or all of the current lines from these mills. They also include the manufacturer's warranties for each style. As you look through these sites, you have to carefully analyze each style you like. Some of the important information (fiber, face weight, performance standards) may not be easily found. Most have customer service phone numbers to call with your questions.

Before you select a carpet, someone must carefully measure your rooms. Are you hiring an independent installer who will also measure for you? Or are you installing the carpet yourself (not recommended)? The carpet width—12 foot, 13 foot 2 inches, or 15 foot—makes a difference when figuring yardage. Does the carpet have a pattern that must be matched? You must figure extra carpet for the pattern match. You must also calculate enough waste. If you come up short, you can't run out and buy another eight yards of carpet the way you can buy another gallon of paint.

*Also keep in mind that you assume all responsibility for the goods received.* Here is a typical disclosure from one of the online sites:

> Once your order arrives in your area, the carrier can give you a 24- to 48-hour advanced call to schedule your delivery. You will need someone to help receive your order and remove it from the delivery truck. It is your responsibility to inspect the condition and number of pieces and make notations before accepting delivery from the freight line. There could be hidden damage that is not visible at time of delivery. If you suspect, but cannot be sure of damage, you should mark the paperwork "Suspected Damage—Exact Amount Unknown."

The disclosure warns you about several important things. They will deliver the carpet roll—weighing several hundred pounds—to your driveway. You are responsible for making sure that even the innermost portion of the roll is undamaged both by *the shipper and by the mill.* You'll wish you had a forklift to take the carpet roll off the truck and get it into your garage or some other place for safe storage. (Hope it's not raining!) Before you cut the carpet for installation, remember that only uncut carpet with a visual defect is covered by the mill warranty before installation. Once you cut it, the carpet is yours, no matter what. That means you need to unroll the entire piece of carpet and inspect it carefully. Where will you do the unrolling and inspection? Ask the online retailer and your installer these questions, unless you are installing it yourself.

And of course, you must find a reputable installer. Hiring someone from Craig's List or through the local newspaper's Services page could be an adventure all by itself. You could search for a Certified Carpet Installer at cfiinstallers.com (Certified Flooring Installers International). Or you could call the local union hall or installer workroom and ask for some names. Then check their credentials and work habits carefully. Read the section below on installation and quiz them. You will have a lot of money tied up in this project. Make sure you are comfortable with your installer.

If you find a "*latent*" defect (one that shows up after the carpet has been installed), most mills require you to notify your eseller in order to begin the claims process. Since you won't have a local retailer to handle the claim, you'll have to do the work yourself. If your claim is denied, you will not have much leverage to force the mill to give your claim a second look. If these thoughts make you uncomfortable, then consider these alternatives.

**Buying from a specialty retailer.** Buying from a local retailer has advantages, too. They assume the shipping and inspection responsibilities for you. Most retail flooring stores are locally owned by someone who lives nearby. These small businesses employ individuals——salespeople, bookkeepers, warehouse personnel—who live in your neighborhood and whose children go to local schools. You help drive the local economy when you shop at a neighborhood retailer. So how do you find the right one?

The best way to find a retailer is through the grapevine. Many small carpet stores are excellent but cannot afford splashy newspaper ads or large spreads in the yellow pages. Larger specialty stores will have a broader selection and will probably have more carpet in stock for immediate delivery. Mills also contribute to advertising budgets for high-volume operations. Most retailers, both small and large, will have shop-at-home services. They may have a special van with most of the styles you'll find in the store, or the dealer will discuss your needs and bring a limited selection of samples to your home. Ask your friends and acquaintances who they have used and from whom they have received superior sales and service. A recommendation from a happy customer is the best advertising for any store. They depend on customer good will to spread the word for them. Try to get at least two names so you can compare value. Value is more than dollar cost. Remember: Pay cheap, get cheap.

Comparing prices alone is an incomplete way to approach your flooring project. Buying from a local retailer gives you access to someone who knows the tastes of the local community. Find out how long they have been in business. How much flooring experience does your salesperson have? If you don't have a good decorating sense, your retailer can help you with interior decorating skills at no additional cost to you. They can help you with styles and colors and make other suggestions as well. An experienced retailer is worth extra money.

A retailer with more experienced installers—or better yet, Certified Carpet Installers—would naturally charge more than a retailer who has a constantly revolving installation crew. Most installers are subcontractors rather than employees of a store. Ask the store manager/owner if the installers they use are employees or are at least subcontractors who have a long working relationship with the store. The last thing you want is an installer who disappears if an installation goes bad.

In retailing, there are many ways for a store to get the best price on a line of carpet, and that affects what you will pay for that carpet. Most specialty carpet stores show qualities and prices from low to high. Does the dealer stock full rolls of a style rather than buying cuts? Did the dealer buy a closeout (last season's patterns)? Did the mill run a special price on a particular pattern or style? Did the dealer buy a large lot and get a lower price? Does the store "private label" some carpets? If they belong to a national franchise or have another way to buy with a large pool of retailers, they can buy some lines at substantial savings and give you great pricing. If you comparison shop, you are likely to find that the same carpet will have different prices at different stores. But look at the installed price, with pad.

Check the warranties. The mills warrant their products only, not installation. Does the retailer have its own warranty, especially for installation? What does the warranty cover, exactly? Some places have a 30-day "If you don't love it, we'll take it back" warranty. Remember, the differences between retailers is in the details. You'll have your carpet for a long time. You'll remember any problems with the carpet job long after you've forgotten the price you paid.

**Buying from a home improvement store.** You could say that buying from a "big box" retailer like Home Depot or Lowes is the modern equivalent to yesterday's buying from a department store. Both sell lots of different things. But the similarity ends there.

Department stores no longer have floor covering departments. The home improvement stores compete with the specialty flooring retailers. Some people find it convenient to buy their carpeting where they buy their plumbing and lumber.

If you decide to shop at a home improvement store, ask your salesperson a lot of questions like you did at the specialty store. Find out about their training; how long have they sold flooring; did they work in a different department and recently begin selling carpet? What are their design skills? You'll see a lot of carpet samples. How much do they know about the fiber types, styles best suited for your needs, and installation? It's your money. Get the answers you need.

Prices can be very attractive. You'll find carpet qualities and prices from low to medium-high. Mills often sell "big box" stores exclusive lines that you won't find anywhere else. These lines might be private labeled to make comparison shopping more difficult. They may sell the same carpet you'll see down the street, but it might also have a private label instead of the manufacturer's label. Stores that sell nationally get volume discounts because they buy in huge quantities.

You need to know that the home improvement stores do not have their own installation crews. They contract with large floor-covering installation companies to do their work. The stores set the installation quality standards, but it is up the contracting company to make sure their crews maintain those standards. If you have an installation problem, you'll complain to the store. But someone from the installation company will handle your complaint.

**Buying through an Interior Designer.** An individual must meet the strict requirements of the American Society of Interior Designers in order to call themselves an Interior Designer and put "ASID" after their name. It takes a lot of training, time, sales experience, and many courses to become an ASID member. Many people call themselves Interior Decorators instead of Interior Designers. They are not the same thing. While there are many fine Decorators with good taste in business, Designers are at a completely different level.

If you want to use a Designer, begin your search by getting referrals. Then find out if the Designer works freelance or for a design studio. You may find a wider selection of carpeting styles with a freelance Designer. Make sure that whomever you interview has a long list of satisfied clients. It is a must to see their finished work firsthand.

You must decide if your tastes and the Designer's ideas mesh. Since you'll be working closely with this individual, your personalities must also be a good fit. Ideally, the working relationship should be like a friendship. Both sides should feel comfortable placing ideas into the project.

Designers usually sell medium- to high-quality carpeting. They have access to mills that can custom dye your carpet and make custom area rugs. They charge one of two ways: They may charge an hourly fee, or they may charge a commission and mark up your selections to cover the cost of their services. It may cost you more, but you'll receive a wide selection of choices and creative, unusual ideas. If your budget has room for an Interior Designer, you should find the one that is right for you.

The installers used by an ASID member are probably the finest craftsmen in your area. They are accustomed to installing both tufted and woven fine-quality floor coverings. They will dress and act professionally. They are skilled at large, unusual installations. Would you like a medallion in the center of your room? Some freestyle hand carving? They can do it all.

## SHOP SMART

If you look regularly at carpet ads in the newspaper, you'll notice a couple of things. First, carpet stores, like most retailers, have "sales" every week. They need to get you in their store and they know that a "SALE" sign gets your attention. Second, the very best time to buy carpet is in the early spring or early fall of each year.

The big yearly U.S. wholesale flooring market, called Surfaces, is held at the end of every January in Las Vegas. All the buyers for the flooring stores go there to see the newest styles and the latest fibers. They order their product lines, make special market purchases, and make purchasing commitments for the coming year. Any savings or reductions found at Surfaces are passed along to consumers as major specials.

By early spring, the new carpets have been shipped by the mills and the retailers are ready to "move some rugs." The housing market begins to move again after the winter doldrums. Springtime is also fix-up time after a long, cold winter. Working in the garden and around the house is almost fun after staying inside for so long. It's time to spruce things up inside and out, and that often means new carpeting.

This is when the flooring merchandisers gear up for their first big sale of the year.

Then, after summer vacations and the start of the school year, people begin to think about the upcoming holiday season. They may notice that their home is looking a little tired and needs some fixing up. This is when the flooring stores typically have their second big sale period of the year. The retailers want to get their cash registers ringing during the fall home-improvement season. They know that once the holiday season arrives, people just want to get their decorations up and enjoy family time.

Mills give their best prices to retailers who buy full rolls in large lots. This means that chain stores or independent stores that are part of a large buying group usually sell at a lower price. But there are exceptions. A small store could buy a "special" from a mill at a very advantageous price. Or a high-volume family-owned store could buy enough to qualify for the best prices. The main point is that you should comparison shop carefully. Do your homework. When you are ready to buy, you'll know it when you see the right carpet at the right price.

Most people aren't in a rush to buy carpet. It is not an "impulse" item. Most people only buy carpet every 7 to 10 years, sometimes much longer. So once you think it might be time to buy carpet "soon," start looking at the carpet ads. You'll probably see the same stores advertising in the paper on a regular basis. If you check their ads, you'll get a good idea of what styles are popular and how much carpet costs these days. Carpet traditionally was priced "per square yard," with nine square feet in a square yard. Carpet is now priced both per square yard and per square foot, so you can easily see how carpet price compares to that of other square-foot-priced floor coverings.

Some stores advertise only their lowest priced carpet as an enticement to get you in the store. Most reputable retailers have a good-better-best choice of products for you. The base carpet is "good." That means it's probably suitable for low-traffic rooms like bedrooms. The next quality is "better." That means it's okay for a living room and dining room or a home with relatively low traffic. The "best" category will work anywhere in your home, even if it is a busy, active home with a lot of traffic.

Often a retailer sells a package with carpet, pad, and installation included. A package could include a special on this year's carpet or a dropped line from last year. Again, there may be a "base" package, a "better" package, and a "best" package. The better and best groups will have better pad and carpet as the price moves up. The installation portion stays the same. Be careful when someone offers "free labor." While the flooring business is very competitive, there is no free anything. The cost of installation must be included somewhere. You'll pay more for one thing in order to get something "free" somewhere else. You *do* get what you pay for. If the labor truly is free, the installation will be only as good as what you have paid for it!

Tip: If you must re-carpet but your budget is tight or you plan on staying in your home for only a short time, you have another alternative. Look for a retailer who sells *mill trials* and/or *seconds or irregular goods*. You'll have to call around. A lot of dealers don't sell trials or irregulars. Mills experiment with new patterns, new fibers, and new colorations of old patterns. While something might look good on a computer screen, only a production run will show the fabric as the consumer sees it. The mill might make several rolls of the new pattern or color, only to discover that it is not as popular in the marketplace as they had hoped. So they sell it as a first-quality mill trial at a special price. You may not find the exact color or pattern you want, but you'll save a lot of money with a mill trial. The mill trials should have the same warranty as a comparable carpet in the mills' running lines.

Seconds, or irregulars, are different. These carpets are not first quality and may not even have a full warranty. Many factors make a carpet second quality. The color of the finished product might vary from the samples, but the carpet is first quality in every other way. The roll might contain streaks or shearing variances. The heat set might not be perfect. The roll width might be narrower than allowed by the mill's standards. The secondary backing might not be properly adhered. Any variance from the mills' first quality standards turns carpet rolls into "seconds." The mills would rather sell these seconds for something instead of dumping them for nothing. So you can buy some potentially inexpensive, good-quality carpet.

When the retailer buys these rolls, they are told by the mill why they are seconds. A reputable dealer will mark the rolls "seconds." If you are interested, you can have the carpet unrolled and inspect it with the dealer. See if there is a color variation from the samples or if there is something wrong that will affect the carpet's performance in your home. Sometimes streaks or dye spots can be cut out during installation. A narrow width might not make any difference if you're installing the carpet in bedrooms. You potentially could save yourself a lot of money if you consider irregulars. Most irregulars do not have a warranty; they are sold "as is." But it might be worth it to you if you can save enough money and still have a new carpet.

## LET'S GO SHOPPING!

Now let's go shopping. I'll be your personal shopper. Together, we'll visit an imaginary carpet store—a composite of stores you'll likely see. We'll look for a good-quality family room carpet and we'll consider color, quality, and price. We know we want a fiber that is tough—the family room gets a lot of traffic. With three kids, a dog, and two cats, spills must clean up easily, too. And it must have a strong warranty against texture change and fading. Of course, whatever we choose must be priced for our budget.

As we walk through the doors, we are greeted by a carpet specialist who is eager to help with our selection. We tell our salesperson that we are only looking at this point. He suggests we look around and familiarize ourselves with the store, then come to him with any questions or requests.

Having a competent salesperson is key to the purchase and installation of carpet. It makes everything so much easier. When choosing a particular designer or salesperson, you must keep in mind that personality is a key factor. The designer-consumer relationship should be like friends working together—easygoing and comfortable. The designer or salesperson should not be too pushy or aggressive and should help guide the decision making.

Of course, knowledge of the product is also important. If the explanations you receive are vague or confusing, talk to someone else. Find someone who knows what is being sold and explains things simply and clearly. Also, look at sales presentation. Reputable retailers have nothing to hide. They are eager to explain their goods and services and wouldn't think about selling you one product and delivering something else—the old bait-and-switch trick. They know their carpets in detail and are proud of their stores. And remember one other thing: Most salespeople are on commission; why give a lot of money to someone you distrust or dislike?

As we look around the store, we see an enormous selection of styles in every color of the rainbow. Cut pile samples are arranged along one side of the main aisle; loop and cut and loop styles along the opposite side. There is also a color wall for us to see. On one wall, various samples are arranged in a color spectrum—reds, oranges, yellows, greens, blues, violets, and purples—to show us the enormous variety available.

Some sample racks are marked "in stock," ready for immediate delivery and installation. Other patterns must be special ordered; they might take 1 to 8 weeks for delivery. The selection could be overwhelming, but because we have already decided on a certain coloration and price range, our choices will be more manageable.

We are looking for a shade of cream. No matter what the common name is, carpet mills have thought up dozens of other descriptive names for the same color: Lamb's Wool, Cocoa Butter, or Creamsicle. It is easier when selecting a color to bring along a swatch of upholstery or drapery fabric that you want to match with your carpet. Ideally, the best way to establish a color scheme is the way you build your wardrobe: You select a dress and choose accessories to go with the dress. For your home, you should select your carpet first and design the rest of the room around the basic color. Of course, you cannot always start from the floor up, so you'll have to match the carpet to a favorite sofa or the drapes. We've brought an arm cover from the family room sofa to help us select the right color. Finding the right color is relatively easy. It is more difficult to find the right quality and fiber type for our family room. Carpets are made in a wide variety of fibers, as well as varying pile heights and densities.

As we look around, we notice that samples of what appears to be the same carpet seems to have three different prices! When we look more closely, we discover that this style is sold in three different face weights with the same colorways offered in each of the weights. A cream sample is pretty close to the cream we're looking for. It's time to look more closely at the labels attached to the back of the samples. The labels will give us a lot of information regarding fiber type, twist level, warranties, and more.

## LABELS

We start by reading the labels on the back of the cut pile cream sample we first selected. (Please note: Some of the information on the labels shown here may be out of date by the time you go shopping.

As explained earlier, this industry is always changing, so manufacturing techniques and warranties change year by year, too.)

Labels are a great source of information. They are also good "talking points" to discuss with your salesperson. They'll give you general information about fiber type, wear and stain warranties, performance, and care. But be sure to get lots of details about each subject from your salesperson. After reading this book, you'll be able to tell right away if your salesperson knows the business.

The first label (Figure 6-1) on the back of the sample gives us a lot of information: the style name, store SKU number, color (Butterscotch!), fiber, width, and pattern repeat.

**Figure 6-1. Carpet label with general information.**

For our purposes, the fiber, width, and pattern repeat are the most important pieces of information on this label. The fiber is Stainmaster Extrabody II® nylon. Based on what we know about carpet fibers, we know that nylon wears well. And Stainmaster® is a leading brand name in stain-resistant carpet fiber. So we know this is a carpet with a strong warranty. The roll of carpet is made in a 12-foot width. That means, if our rooms are wider than 12 feet, we'll have seams somewhere. And since we'll have seams, the installer will have to measure for extra carpet to allow for the proper pattern match. So we'll have to buy more carpet of this style than if we choose a style with no pattern. All useful information!

Next, we see a label (Figure 6-2) explaining that this particular Stainmaster® nylon is a "green" fiber because it is made partially with castor bean oil, a renewable resource. We also see that Stainmaster®

nylon is type 6.6 nylon. So once the carpet needs replacing, it is easily recyclable; "green" is good!

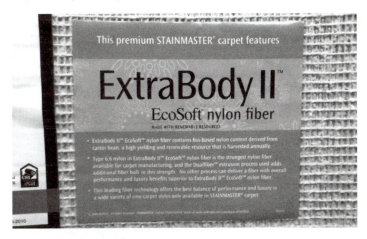

**Figure 6-2. "Green" nylon label.**

Picking another carpet sample from a different rack, we find several labels on the back. We see a "private" label (Figure 6-3). In this case, the national franchise, Abbey Carpet and Floor, sells a carpet line under its name instead of showing you the manufacturer's name. Private labels can save you a lot of money. It's like buying the drugstore brand instead of the "national" brand.

National chains like Abbey Carpet can have mills make an "exclusive" style or quality for them. Because of large-scale buying, a franchise like Abbey can buy an exclusive style at the "right" price and pass the savings along to you. Or the chain might just put its brand on a current style that competitors also sell. Because the chain can buy in such quantities, the mill gives it the best possible wholesale price, and it can beat its competitors' retail price. The warranties are the same—in fact, sometimes a franchise puts a better warranty on its carpet lines to enhance the value of your purchase.

This particular private label gives you complete information: Style name, color, fiber (Stainmaster!), width, and pattern. You also see all the warranty information for wear, stains, and performance/texture retention. There is a little information on vacuuming, static control, colorfastness, and indoor air quality. Again, one label includes a lot of general information. Discuss any details with your salesperson.

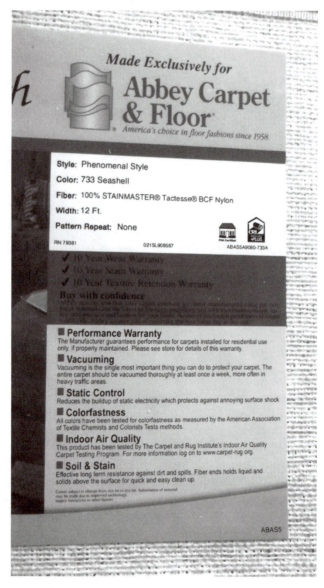

**Made Exclusively for**

# Abbey Carpet & Floor®

*America's choice in floor fashions since 1958.*

**Style:** Phenomenal Style

**Color:** 733 Seashell

**Fiber:** 100% STAINMASTER® Tactesse® BCF Nylon

**Width:** 12 Ft.

**Pattern Repeat:** None

RN 79381          0215L908587          ABAS5A9080-733A

✓ 10 Year Wear Warranty
✓ 10 Year Stain Warranty
✓ 10 Year Texture Retention Warranty

**Buy with confidence**

**■ Performance Warranty**
The Manufacturer guarantees performance for carpets installed for residential use only, if properly maintained. Please see store for details of this warranty.

**■ Vacuuming**
Vacuuming is the single most important thing you can do to protect your carpet. The entire carpet should be vacuumed thoroughly at least once a week, more often in heavy traffic areas.

**■ Static Control**
Reduces the buildup of static electricity which protects against annoying surface shock

**■ Colorfastness**
All colors have been tested for colorfastness as measured by the American Association of Textile Chemists and Colorists Tests methods.

**■ Indoor Air Quality**
This product has been tested by The Carpet and Rug Institute's Indoor Air Quality Carpet Testing Program. For more information log on to www.carpet-rug.org.

**■ Soil & Stain**
Effective long term resistance against dirt and spills. Fiber ends holds liquid and solids above the surface for quick and easy clean up.

Colors subject to change from dye lot to dye lot. Substitution of material may be made due to improved technology, supply limitations or other factors

ABAS5

**Figure 6-3. Private label.**

When we turn over another sample, we find a very helpful label. This one gives a durability rating (Figure 6-4). We know some textures and styles wear better than others. This label explains in detail how well this carpet performs using a standardized wear test. Carpets are subjected, under simulated conditions, to 20,000 footsteps. The results of this test are the carpet's performance or durability ratings. This detailed rating shows you the yarn weight, yarn twist, density, and surface finish. This manufacturer isn't afraid to tell you how well this carpet will hold up!

A different carpet sample (Figure 6-5) also has a performance rating, but without any detail. It puts the above factors—yarn weight, twist, density, and surface finish—into one number for you. That's good if you have a short attention span!

Looking at yet another carpet sample, we find a label explaining the "Features and Benefits" of this carpet (Figure 6-6). We see this carpet is made by Shaw Industries, the largest flooring manufacturer in the world. The label has a lot of helpful facts. This style has a 10-year warranty against manufacturing defects. This is important because carpets typically have a 1-year warranty for manufacturing defects. The industry thinking is that manufacturing problems will show up during the first year the carpet is in use. But as an inspector, I can tell you that sometimes a defect is not noticed during the first year. So this coverage is exceptional.

A 10-year stain-resistance and 10-year texture-retention warranty are excellent. "FHA approved" sounds good but doesn't mean anything to you. FHA-approved carpeting can be a low grade. A 30-day satisfaction guarantee might come in handy—if your carpet shows footprints but you weren't expecting any, for example.

The 10-year warranty against backing wrinkles really falls under the 10-year warranty against defects. The "no wrinkle" clause protects you against backing delamination. But what's really interesting is the backing itself (Figure 6-7). Shaw developed the SoftBac® secondary backing to visually differentiate itself from its competitors. Polypropylene backings are coarse. A careless installer will mar paint by rubbing a carpet back against a painted surface. So Shaw developed the Softbac for carpeting. It is a thin, felt-like fabric that truly makes the secondary backing soft. And it's something you can see. It is a value-added material. It really works as advertised.

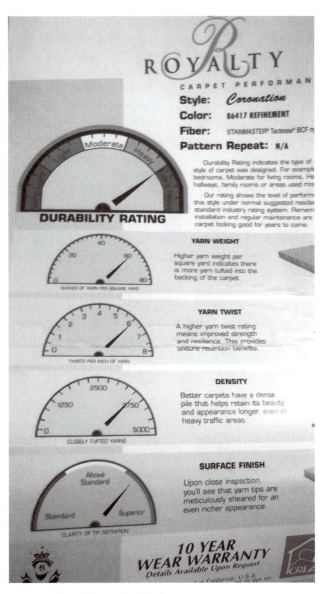

Figure 6-4. Durability rating label.

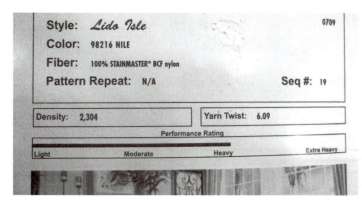

Figure 6-5. Performance rating label.

## FEATURES AND BENEFITS

### 10-YEAR QUALITY ASSURANCE WARRANTY
This warranty certifies that your Shaw carpet will be free of manufacturing defects for a period of 10 years.

### 10-YEAR STAIN RESISTANCE WARRANTY
This warranty certifies that your Shaw carpet will remain stain resistant to most household food and beverage substances for 10 years.

### 10-YEAR TEXTUREGARD® WARRANTY
This Shaw TEXTUREGARD® carpet will not exhibit significant loss of texture from foot traffic for a period of 10 years.

### FHA APPROVED
This Shaw carpet meets or exceeds the minimum standards set by bulletin UM-44D for use in projects for the FHA and HUD.

### 30 DAY CUSTOMER SATISFACTION
If you are not completely satisfied with this Shaw carpet, we will replace your carpet with one of comparable value, excluding charges (such as labor) which relate to the replacement.

**SoftBac** SOFTBAC® PLATINUM
**PLATINUM** This Shaw carpet features SoftBac® Platinum, a revolutionary backing system that offers a 10-year no-wrinkle guarantee.

**color logic** COLOR LOGIC™ color lines
broader, richer, warmer are broader, richer, warmer, and coordinate beautifully with stone, wood and ceramic.

Display Sequence: 0
25664P01 11-2-2006

Figure 6-6. Features and benefits label.

**Figure 6-7. SoftBac (Shaw proprietary secondary backing).**

Secondary backings are what you see when you turn a carpet over. If you look at several different carpet samples, you'll begin to notice the different qualities of the secondary backings. Some have the warp and weft threads relatively far apart. Some are very close together. The backing qualities are determined by "pic" count (Figures 6-8, 6-9, and 6-10). The pic count is the number of widthwise (weft) threads in an inch of fabric. The pic count can be 3, 5, 7, 9, or 11. The mills know that most people don't pay attention to the carpet back. This is one area where they can "economize" and get away with it. But a better back helps the carpet hold up better under traffic. If your final choices are equal in every way except the backing, take the carpet with the better backing. If a mill is saving pennies where you can see their savings, are they cutting corners where you can't see it?

Let's look at other samples and see what we can learn from their labels. Here is label from the Carpet and Rug Institute explaining indoor air quality issues (Figure 6-11). Carpet, like many items found in your home, used to emit VOCs (volatile organic compounds) like formaldehyde. All the "bad" chemicals have been removed from carpeting as well as flooring adhesives. You'll still notice a new carpet smell. But the odor will go away in a few days. This label warns people with high sensitivity to odors to take precautions after the carpet is installed.

Another private label (Figure 6-12) shows that the carpet is made by Mohawk using face yarns of Smartstrand fiber, the newest type of fiber. The label explains the wear, stain, and performance warranties, among other things. We notice that the warranties are as good as Stainmaster's warranties. The carpet industry is competitive, indeed.

Figure 6-8. Low-pic-count secondary backing.

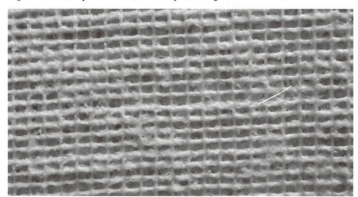

Figure 6-9. Medium–pic-count secondary backing.

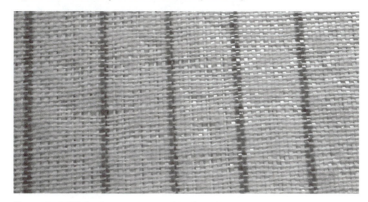

Figure 6-10. High-pic-count secondary backing.

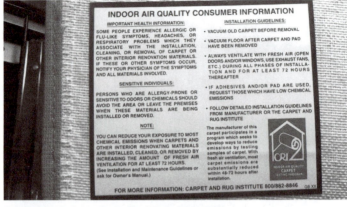

**INDOOR AIR QUALITY CONSUMER INFORMATION**

IMPORTANT HEALTH INFORMATION:

SOME PEOPLE EXPERIENCE ALLERGIC OR FLU-LIKE SYMPTOMS, HEADACHES, OR RESPIRATORY PROBLEMS WHICH THEY ASSOCIATE WITH THE INSTALLATION, CLEANING, OR REMOVAL OF CARPET OR OTHER INTERIOR RENOVATION MATERIALS. IF THESE OR OTHER SYMPTOMS OCCUR, NOTIFY YOUR PHYSICIAN OF THE SYMPTOMS AND ALL MATERIALS INVOLVED.

SENSITIVE INDIVIDUALS:

PERSONS WHO ARE ALLERGY-PRONE OR SENSITIVE TO ODORS OR CHEMICALS SHOULD AVOID THE AREA OR LEAVE THE PREMISES WHEN THESE MATERIALS ARE BEING INSTALLED OR REMOVED.

NOTE:

YOU CAN REDUCE YOUR EXPOSURE TO MOST CHEMICAL EMISSIONS WHEN CARPETS AND OTHER INTERIOR RENOVATING MATERIALS ARE INSTALLED, CLEANED, OR REMOVED BY INCREASING THE AMOUNT OF FRESH AIR VENTILATION FOR AT LEAST 72 HOURS. (See Installation and Maintenance Guidelines or ask for Owner's Manual.)

INSTALLATION GUIDELINES:

• VACUUM OLD CARPET BEFORE REMOVAL

• VACUUM FLOOR AFTER CARPET AND PAD HAVE BEEN REMOVED

• ALWAYS VENTILATE WITH FRESH AIR (OPEN DOORS AND/OR WINDOWS, USE EXHAUST FANS, ETC.) DURING ALL PHASES OF INSTALLATION AND FOR AT LEAST 72 HOURS THEREAFTER

• IF ADHESIVES AND/OR PAD ARE USED, REQUEST THOSE WHICH HAVE LOW CHEMICAL EMISSIONS

• FOLLOW DETAILED INSTALLATION GUIDELINES FROM MANUFACTURER OR THE CARPET AND RUG INSTITUTE

The manufacturer of this carpet participates in a program which seeks to develop ways to reduce emissions by testing samples of carpet. With fresh air ventilation, most carpet emissions are substantially reduced within 48-72 hours after installation.

FOR MORE INFORMATION: CARPET AND RUG INSTITUTE 800/882-8846

**Figure 6-11. Indoor-air-quality information label.**

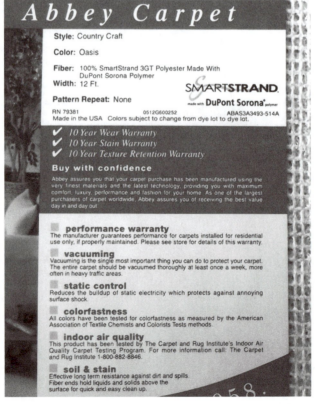

*Abbey Carpet*

Style: Country Craft

Color: Oasis

Fiber: 100% SmartStrand 3GT Polyester Made With DuPont Sorona Polymer

Width: 12 Ft.

Pattern Repeat: None

SMARTSTRAND.
made with DuPont Sorona polymer

RN 79381        0512G600252        ABAS3A3493-514A
Made in the USA   Colors subject to change from dye lot to dye lot.

✔ *10 Year Wear Warranty*
✔ *10 Year Stain Warranty*
✔ *10 Year Texture Retention Warranty*

**Buy with confidence**

Abbey assures you that your carpet purchase has been manufactured using the very finest materials and the latest technology, providing you with maximum comfort, luxury, performance and fashion for your home. As one of the largest purchasers of carpet worldwide, Abbey assures you of receiving the best value day in and day out

**performance warranty**
The manufacturer guarantees performance for carpets installed for residential use only, if properly maintained. Please see store for details of this warranty.

**vacuuming**
Vacuuming is the single most important thing you can do to protect your carpet. The entire carpet should be vacuumed thoroughly at least once a week, more often in heavy traffic areas.

**static control**
Reduces the buildup of static electricity which protects against annoying surface shock.

**colorfastness**
All colors have been tested for colorfastness as measured by the American Association of Textile Chemists and Colorists Tests methods.

**indoor air quality**
This product has been tested by The Carpet and Rug Institute's Indoor Air Quality Carpet Testing Program. For more information call: The Carpet and Rug Institute 1-800-882-8846.

**soil & stain**
Effective long term resistance against dirt and spills. Fiber ends hold liquids and solids above the surface for quick and easy clean up.

**Figure 6-12. Private label with Smartstrand® fiber.**

And yet another label (Figure 6-13) tells us the benefits of Wear-Dated® nylon, one of Stainmaster's® competitors. It also has a strong wear, stain, and soil warranty.

If all this seems like it is too much to understand, don't worry. The information you've just read has prepared you for the next step. If you have a budget, you are now ready to work with a trained designer or salesperson. They will help you make sense of everything—color, styles, and quality. Just work with someone you like who is knowledgeable. You will enjoy the choices ahead of you. Then, after you've made your selections and the carpet is installed, you can sit back, relax, and enjoy the comfort of your newly improved home!

**Figure 6-13. Wear-Dated® nylon label.**

# 7

# CARPET INSTALLATION

Now we come to a topic that is almost ignored when you buy carpet: the installation of the new carpet in your home. You've probably had someone come to your home to measure the rooms—maybe the shop owner, your salesperson, or an installer. At this point, you know how much carpet you'll need and how much it's going to cost. Most installers add an additional 10 percent yardage because there are always waste and surprises. This is standard practice. Also, a roll is considered 12 feet wide, even if the actual measurement is as narrow as 11 feet 10 inches. You have a choice to make. Should you do-it-yourself, or should you let a professional installer do it for you?

## DO-IT-YOURSELF INSTALLATION

Do-it-yourself carpet installation is one of the hardest projects you'll ever try. I don't recommend it. Anything more than a single room can turn into a nightmare. Mistakes are very expensive. Tools are specialized (Figure 7-1) and hard to find at most rental stores. Carpet rolls are large and very heavy. Laying tackstrip is more difficult than it looks, and even professionals have trouble with seams. And, of course, stretching the carpet properly over the pad can be backbreaking.

If you think you're ready for a challenge, gather up your tools and read this section. Otherwise, what is included below is meant as a primer for those of us who want to watch professionals do their job and know that it's being done correctly. After you read this chapter, you will know as much as, or more than, the team installing the carpet in your home.

So have your retailer or decorator send out their installation team, sit back, and enjoy the show.

**Figure 7-1a. Carpet installation tool: Twin cutter.**

**Figure 7-1b. Carpet installation tool: Utility knife.**

**Figure 7-1c. Carpet installation tool: Wall tucker (wide-bladed tool).**

**Figure 7-1d. Carpet installation tool: Walltrimmer.**

## PROFESSIONAL INSTALLATION

### Measuring

As mentioned earlier, you must have the areas you will carpet accurately measured. This is not as easy as it sounds. Most carpet comes in standard 12-foot widths, but many rooms are wider than twelve feet. You can't measure a room, take length times width, and come up with the correct square footage. You have to take the extra carpet from rooms narrower than twelve feet and put the extra fabric into the rooms that are wider than twelve feet, or cut the needed carpet from the end of the roll. You also have to make sure that the carpet pile from cut pieces runs in the same direction as the rest of the carpet.

Patterned carpet presents an extra piece to this puzzle. Patterns must be matched at the seams. A label on the back of the carpet sample will tell you the "repeat" of the pattern—so many inches lengthwise between a pattern repeat, so many inches widthwise between a pattern repeat. Extra carpet must be added to the overall room measurements to allow for the pattern repeats.

Whoever measures your home—the retailer, an estimator, or an installer—should make a seam diagram. This is important because it will show you where the seams will be placed. In fact, a seam diagram should be discussed when you buy the carpet. Have your retailer agree to show you the diagram and go over it with you so you can approve where the seams go. If your retailer doesn't use seam diagrams or won't agree to show it to you, *go somewhere else*! I can't tell you how many times I've heard, "I didn't know the seam would go there!" or "I didn't know there would be so many seams!" or "The salesman said the seam would go *there*, but the installer put it *here* instead!" Avoid the headaches. Get a seam diagram and approve it with your signature before the carpet is ordered. Enough things can go wrong during an installation; surprise seams shouldn't be among them.

Seam placement is important because seamed areas are usually among the first places to show wear. Seams should be kept to a minimum. They should run the length of the carpeted areas, out of traffic lanes when possible, and away from doorways. Seam placement also determines how much carpet you'll need to complete the job. You don't want to come up several yards short!

Most rooms can be laid out in two directions. One way has fewer seams and leaves more waste. The other direction has more seams and less waste. Since many jobs laid out with minimum seaming only use a few extra yards of material, it's best to have extra scrap rather than more seams.

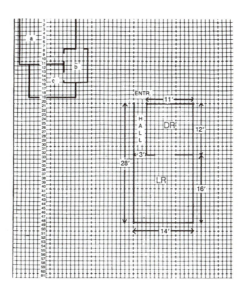

**Figure 7-2. A floor plan showing all measurements.**

In our example floor plan (Figure 7-2), two rooms and a hall are measured for installation and are plotted on graph paper to keep proportions and measurements accurate. The living room is 14 feet wide and 16 feet long. The dining room is 11 feet wide and 12 feet long, with a 3-foot-wide and 12-foot-long hallway next to it. The living room's total width of 14 feet is multiplied by the total length of the combined living and dining room's 28 feet, for a total of 392 square feet. Dividing this figure by 9 gives the square yards, which is 43.5. This is not the amount you need to order. Because the total job is wider than the 12 foot width of the carpet, you must calculate the fill pieces and 10 percent waste into the total figure. To have enough carpet to do the job neatly, you must start with a piece of carpet a minimum of 12 feet x 36 feet (Figure 7-3). This totals 48 square yards, or 432 square feet. Cutting a piece 12 x 28 feet, 6 inches gives enough to cover the full length of all three areas, with a piece 12 x 7 feet, 6 inches left for cutting into the 3 x 7 feet, 6 inch pieces needed to fill in (fill pieces!) the room (Figure 7-4). There is enough carpet to provide extra in case the rooms are not square.

## A Word to the Wise

Like any other craft, carpet installers' skills vary widely. Installers learn their craft by starting as apprentices with a crew. An apprentice might only take up the old carpet and carry tools at first, but slowly learns by watching the others perform their jobs. In this way the apprentice learns to become an installer. But hold on! What if the apprentice learns *bad* installation techniques? The apprentice doesn't know any difference between bad and good installations. I have seen apprentices learn from installers who have been doing things the wrong way for thirty years! How do you know that the crew who shows up to install your carpet (after you worked so hard to haul out the furniture!) knows what they're doing? How do you know that the head of your installation crew wasn't yesterday's apprentice? A lot of retailers hire the lowest bidder and don't even bother to check the finished job—until there's a complaint! The answer is a "Certified Flooring Installer!" Never heard of one? Well, they are out there. They have taken time off work (at their own cost, since installers are self-employed) to attend multi-day classes, usually out of town. They must pass written tests and actually install carpet. They'll have a certificate proving that they are certified professionals and know their stuff. They usually charge more for their work, but they are worth any difference in cost! I would compare the difference between an ordinary installer and a certified installer to a "backyard" car mechanic and a certified car mechanic.

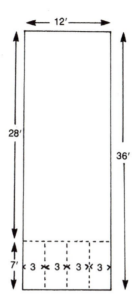

**Figure 7-3. Cutting 12-foot-wide carpet to fit a 14-foot-wide room.**

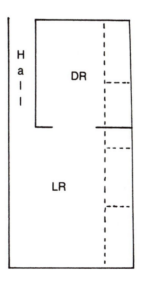

**Figure 7-4. A seam diagram for Figure 7-2 floor plan.
Dotted lines indicate seams.**

You'll have to ask your retailer if the installers he uses are certified. If he insists that his installers are as good as Certified Flooring Installers and he guarantees their work, ask him why he doesn't use Certified Flooring Installers. You'll remember how your back ached after you emptied your house to prepare for the installation. Do you really want to do it again when a non-certified crew makes a mess of your expensive carpet—and maybe your home? If you are the type who thinks that cheap equals good, then you'll be happy with whomever shows up to install your carpet.

### Installing Tackstrip

Once you have signed off on the seam diagram, your retailer will order the agreed-upon amount of carpet and pad. When the materials are delivered, the actual installation begins. The installers will remove the old carpet and pad. Sometimes they will leave the existing tackstrip (also called tackless strip) around the room perimeters. If the rooms have never had installed carpet, the installers will add tackstrip around all room perimeters and floor vents (Figures 7-5, 7-6). Stairs are also tackstripped at the bottom of the riser and the back of the tread.

**Figure 7-5. Putting down tackstrip.**

**Figure 7-6. Tackstrip around floor vents.**

In the "old" days, carpet was tacked directly to the subfloor. The carpet would dimple wherever it was tacked. Tackless strip was invented to provide a smooth, tight installation without the dimples. The *tackstrips* are thin strips of wood, 1 to 1¾ inches wide, which are pre-nailed with two to three rows of gripper pins set at a 20 to 30-degree angle. The pins are pointed towards the wall. The 4-foot lengths are nailed to wood floors and glued or nailed to concrete floors. The strips are lightweight and easily trimmed for tight areas or upholstery work. The carpet is stretched over the pad, then hooked and held in place under tension by the gripper pins.

It is not always smart to use the old tackstrip when replacing carpet. The strip is nailed a certain distance from the wall based on the thickness of the carpet. If the total thickness of the carpet is ¾ inch, for example, the strip is placed ¼ to ⅜ inch away from the wall (Figure 7-7). If the old carpet was quite different in thickness from what you're now installing, the new carpet might not wedge between the strip and the wall properly. The carpet might not stay stretched on the tackstrip pins. If the strip is in good condition and is the correct distance from the wall, it is perfectly all right to use it. But if the installers must replace it, don't worry. Tackstrip is inexpensive and built into the installation cost. You won't get a refund if you reuse the old strip.

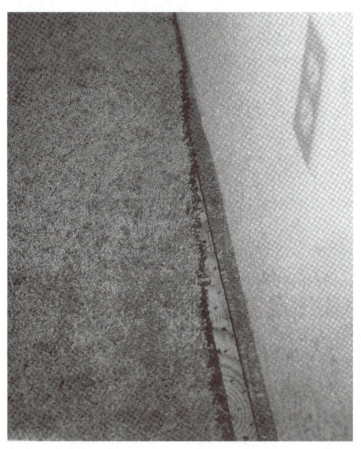

**Figure 7-7. The carpet fits between the tackstrip and the wall.**

Double rows of standard strip or three-row architectural/commercial strip are used if the carpet will get extra-heavy use, if it is installed over a concrete floor, or if the carpet "run" is over 30 feet. (Figure 7-8).

There's one other thing to consider when reusing old tackstrip. The gripper pins come in different lengths. The installer must decide, based on the carpet thickness and type of backing, which length is right for your carpet. A "J" pin ($^5/_{32}$ inch) is used for low profile and woven carpets. A "D" pin ($^3/_{16}$ inch) is used for a dense pile carpet. An "E" pin ($^7/_{32}$ inch) is the most common length. A "C" pin (¼ inch) is used with a rough or thick backing. Long pins sticking through a thin carpet will puncture barefoot toes. That really takes away from a newly carpeted floor!

**Figure 7-8. Use double tackstrip on a concrete subfloor.**

## Installing Pad

Once the tackstrip is installed, the pad is laid down (Figure 7-9). Most underlayments have a smooth or slippery surface on one side only. This is the "up" side. The slick surface allows the carpet backing to slide smoothly over the pad when the carpet is stretched. Most pads come in 4- or 6-foot widths, or drops, with two or three drops equaling one width of carpet. The drops should be as close together as possible, using the fewest possible cuts, in the longest lengths possible. Ideally, the cushion seams should be at right angles to the carpet seams. If this is not possible, the pad seams should be at least six inches from any carpet seams. The underlayment is trimmed up against the tackstrip. The pad should be stapled to wood subfloors or glued to concrete floors with non-flammable pad adhesive. All cushion seams, except for fiber cushions, should be taped with cushion tape. Once the pad is down, the easiest part of the installation is finished.

**Figure 7-9. Laying carpet pad.**

## CARPET INSTALLATION

While the old carpet is removed and tackstrip and pad are installed, the carpet is acclimating. This means that the carpet is "getting used to" the atmospheric conditions in your home. This is especially important if you live in a cold climate. Carpet is mostly plastic of one type or another. Plastic is stiff and hard when it is cold. The carpet must adjust to the interior climate where it will "live" for the rest of its life. If it's cold outside and the heat is off in your home, the carpet will not stretch properly during installation. Once you turn on the heat, the stiff carpet will relax and stretch. Then you'll have wrinkles, and the carpet will need a re-stretch. So make sure the temperature and humidity inside your home are at a normal level so the carpet will install properly. If you are installing the carpet when it is hot and humid outside, you'll need to run the air conditioner to normalize your home's interior. The mills like you to allow 12 to 24 hours as an acclimation period.

Everyone agrees that the most important, and most difficult, part of the installation is the cutting, seaming, and stretching of the carpet itself. The installers use specialized tools for this part of the job. They also need skill and patience to complete this part of the installation so that they leave you with a beautifully carpeted home.

Carpet is made in long rolls, often 100 feet or more. Today, the standard width is 12 feet, although a carpet as narrow as 11 feet, 10 inches meets the minimum industry standard. (Some styles are made in 13-foot, 2-inch, or 15-foot widths.) Based on the seam diagram, the installers will cut the correct amount from the roll in one piece. If more than one roll is needed for your installation, then consecutive *dye lots* (rolls all of the same dye batch) are needed. Professional installers often do preliminary cutting in a workroom or warehouse and bring the partially cut roll to the job site for final cutting and fitting. They'll sometimes cut the full roll in your driveway instead. If you do it yourself, you will have to cut the carpet roll in your driveway.

## Cutting the Carpet

It is most important to make clean, straight cuts, with a carpet knife. The carpet can be cut from the back or the face, depending on the carpet construction. A long straight edge helps to make good cuts. When cutting and seaming carpet, installers include extra fabric for overlaps of a couple of inches along the walls and seams. (Figure 7-10). This prevents the installers from coming up short when the pieces are put together. The extra fabric is later trimmed away. This is why a room can't be measured down to the last inch, and why you must figure waste into the final measurement. Once the carpet is cut, the installers will lay the pieces out in their correct places.

All fabric, including carpet, has a sweep or direction in which the nap lays. When piecing carpet together, it is *most* important that all pieces lay in the same direction. A piece of carpet that has been turned in relation to the rest of the installation will appear to have a different color than the carpet that surrounds it.

**Figure 7-10. Carpet overlap at a wall.**

It's easy for an installer to keep from turning pieces the wrong way. When the carpet is turned face down, the length of the carpet backing has arrows printed along one side that point "down" the pile. The installer uses a felt-tip pen to draw arrows on any blank sections cut from the roll to indicate the pile direction. When the installer seams pieces together, either when adding fill pieces in one room or when seaming between two rooms, he checks the arrows and makes sure that he lays the carpet so the nap of all the pieces runs in the same direction.

The pile direction always runs "down" stairs because the carpet wears better. Otherwise, the direction of the pile in a given room or area depends on where you have decided to place the seams.

All rolls of carpet, whether woven or tufted, have a selvedge along each side that must be trimmed away. The *selvedge* (Figure 7-11) is a raw, weak edge of unfilled backing material that extends beyond the normal width of the carpet. Some mills trim off the selvedge before delivering the finished carpet, others do not. The installer will trim off any selvedge. He can't *side seam* the carpet—make seams along the lengthwise edge—until the weak selvedge is removed. (Seams made across the 12-foot width are called *cross seams.*)

Figure 7-11. The raw selvedge must be trimmed prior to seaming.

Once the carpet is trimmed, cut to size, and laid out properly, it is ready for seaming. The first thing to understand about seaming carpet is that *there is no such thing as an invisible seam.* Carpet seams may either be *hand sewn* or hot-melt taped, also called *hot-taping* or *hot seaming.* While it is preferable to hand sew all woven goods, most installers hot tape these seams. Tufted fabrics seam well, whether hand sewn or hot-taped.

Remember when I urged you to hire a Certified Floorcovering Installer? Correctly seaming carpets is technically difficult. It is extremely important to do it right the first time. It is easy for an installer to "cheat" on seaming techniques. You might not see the difference right away. But you *will* have problems in a month or in a year. This is one area where a Certified Floorcovering Installer really makes a difference.

## Seaming Woven Carpet

Many woven fabrics ravel badly along all cut edges, including where it is tucked along walls. The installer applies a thin coat of quick drying liquid adhesive along all the cut edges where the backing and face yarns meet. This includes around room perimeters and where pieces are joined. *Seam sealing* locks in the yarns to keep them from raveling.

After the sealer has dried, the carpet is ready for seaming. The two pieces to be joined are turned backside up. They are cross-stitched together at three to four stitches per inch using a straight needle and waxed linen thread (Figure 7-12).

The installer begins sewing in the center of the seam for patterned carpet and works towards the ends. He must be careful not to catch any face yarns in the stitching or the yarns will be pulled down and make puckers along the seam. As additional protection against premature wear, liquid latex is applied over the stitching itself.

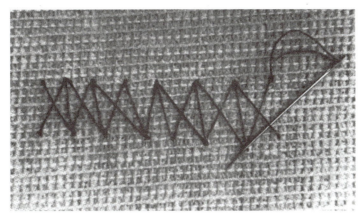

Figure 7-12. A hand-sewn seam.

Woven carpeting is also installed using a hot-melt glue-tape system slightly different from the type used for tufted carpet. The difference is that, because the backing of woven carpet is corrugated, there is more thermoplastic glue on this tape. The extra glue "grabs" the rough backing better. Hot-melt seaming is explained in detail in the Tufted Carpet Installation section later in this chapter.

When all the seams are finished, the carpet is turned over and is stretched in over the tackstrip using a knee kicker (Figure 7-13) and power stretcher (Figure 7-14). The stretching sequence differs, depending on the type of woven carpet used. After you read this section on installation, you'll probably be glad that you decided to let professionals install your carpet!

**Figure 7-13. Knee kicker.**

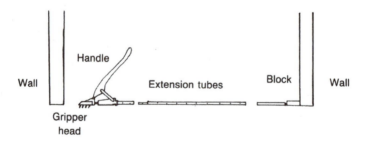

**Figure 7-14. Power stretcher.**

## Stretching the Carpet

The *knee kicker* is a tool with a pinned plate on one end connected to a short (approximately 18-inch) section of adjustable metal tubing. The opposite end has a padded cushion that the installer bumps using the leg just above the knee. The kicker is not used to stretch the carpet except in small areas like a closet and on stairs. Using a kicker begins the installation process by positioning the carpet on the tackstrip pins. The head of the knee kicker is placed a few inches from the wall. The knee kicker uses *gripper pins* to slide the carpet over the tackstrip along a wall. When the kicker is removed from the carpet, it hooks on the angled pins of the strip as the carpet slides backwards.

The pinned plate is adjustable. When the longer, coarser gripper pins are retracted, the immediate underside of the plate is exposed. It is made from closely spaced, fine pins—more like needles. These *nap-grip* pins are used on all loop piles. The coarser gripper pins extend past the nap-grip pins for use on cut pile and cut and loop piles.

The extendable gripper pins are adjusted for the thickness of the carpet. They grip the backing without breaking it. If the teeth are not set deeply enough, they do not grip the backing properly and can tear it. Tufts sticking above the carpet surface along the room edges are a sure sign of kicker tears. Improperly adjusted pins have torn the carpet backing. If the teeth are set too deeply, they snag the padding and the carpet doesn't slide.

The kicker is gripped by the neck behind the head. Downward pressure is applied to the head while the kicker pad is bumped using the leg just above the knee. As the kicker head is moved over the tackstrip, the downward pressure pushes the carpet onto the gripper pins of the tackstrip. A stair tool or hammer head slid over the carpet pile pushes it firmly onto the pins. This makes the overlapped carpet stick up at a 90 degree angle above the gully between the strip and the wall. A wide bladed tool (Figure 7-15) is used to tuck the overlap into the gully. This holds the carpet fast while it is stretched.

**Figure 7-15. Wide-bladed tool for tucking carpet.**

## Using the Power Stretcher

A *power stretcher,* like the knee kicker, has an adjustable pinned gripper plate, tubular extensions, a padded end, and a lever system that multiplies the installers' applied stretching force. Once properly adjusted, the stretcher head is placed 3 to 5 inches from the wall. The tubes are extended across the room to the opposite wall. A wooden block is sometimes placed between the padded end and the wall. This helps distribute energy across a wider area.

As the handle is slowly pumped a few times, the carpet stretches across the room. A power stretcher moves a carpet about 1 inch per 10 feet of carpet length. (This figure varies with the type of construction and the quality of the carpet.) When the handle is held down and locked, the carpet is held in place. The knee kicker holds the carpet down behind the tackstrip while the stretcher handle is raised. This releases the pressure from the stretcher head, and the carpet pulls back and down onto the tackstrip pins.

## Stretching Wilton and Velvet Weaves

These weaves have a soft backing and can be stretched in any direction. The installers begin by anchoring the carpet on the tackstrip at corner A (Figure 7-16).

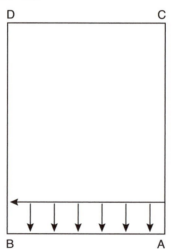

**Figure 7-16. Installing Wilton and Velvet weave carpet.**
**Step 1: Power-stretch from corner A to corner B and hook.**
**Use straight knee kicks to hook the carpet onto wall AB.**

Then they power-stretch from A and hook the carpet to corner B. Using straight kicks with the knee kicker, they hook the carpet along the width A to B. Then they power-stretch along wall A to C and hook the carpet onto the strip at corner C. They again use straight kicks to hook the carpet along the length from A to C (Figure 7-17).

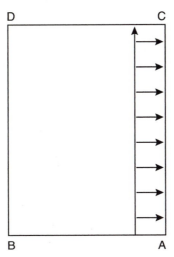

**Figure 7-17. Installing Wilton and Velvet weave carpet.**
**Step 2: Power stretch from corner A to C and hook.**
**Use straight knee kicks to hook carpet onto wall AC.**

Next, they position the padded end of the power stretcher against wall AB 2 or 3 feet from corner B. The stretcher head is placed in corner D and the carpet is power stretched at a 15-degree angle and hooked in corner D (Figure 7-18). The pad of the power stretcher is put in corner A and the head in corner B. They begin the power stretch here and move down the room using straight stretches every 2 to 3 feet, from wall AB to wall CD. They hook the carpet onto the tackstrip after each power stretch (Figure 7-19). Returning to corner A, they place the pad of the stretcher here and the head of the stretcher in corner C. Stretching the length of the carpet along the wall AB every 2 or 3 feet hooks the carpet onto the tackstrip of wall CD (Figure 7-20). The carpet is now completely stretched in. They'll finish by trimming around the perimeter, then tuck the edge of the carpet into the gully between the tackstrip and the wall.

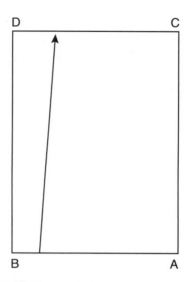

**Figure 7-18. Installing Wilton and Velvet weave carpet. Step 3: Power stretch from corner B at a 15-degree angle to corner D and hook.**

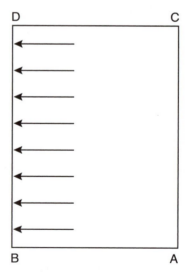

**Figure 7-19. Installing Wilton and Velvet weave carpet. Step 4: Use straight power stretches from wall AC to hook carpet along wall BD.**

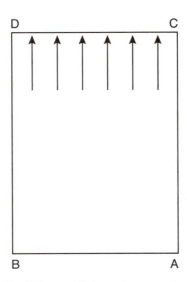

**Figure 7-20. Installing Wilton and Velvet weave carpet. Step 5: Use straight power stretches from wall BA to hook the carpet along wall DC.**

## Stretching Axminster Carpet

Axminster carpet is the only weave that just stretches lengthwise, so it is stretched differently from the other constructions. It is easy to recognize Axminster because the pattern is woven through the back (Figures 7-21 and 7-22). The installers begin by anchoring the carpet in corner A (Figure 7-23). They put the pad of the stretcher in corner A and the head in corner C. They power-stretch the length from A to C and hook the carpet on the tackstrip at corner C. Then they use the kicker and straight-kick along wall AC to hook the carpet on the strip along this wall.

Next, they use the kicker to pull and hook the carpet onto the tackstrip at corner B. Using straight kicks, they hook the carpet onto the strip along wall AB (Figure 7-24). Then they place the stretcher pad in corner B and, putting the head in corner D, power-stretch the entire length of wall BD and hook the carpet to the strip in corner D (Figure 7-25). Then they move the stretcher pad to corner A and the head in corner C.

They power-stretch the length of the carpet and hook the fabric to the tackstrip along wall CD. Then they move the stretcher pad every

2 or 3 feet along wall AB and stretch along the entire wall CD, hooking the carpet on the strip pins as they go (Fig 7-26). They use straight kicks with the knee kicker along the entire wall BD to hook the carpet to the tackstrip (Figure 7-27). The carpet is now stretched in. They'll finish by trimming around the perimeter, then tuck the edge of the carpet into the gully between the tackstrip and the wall.

Figure 7-21. The patterned pile of an Axminster weave carpet.

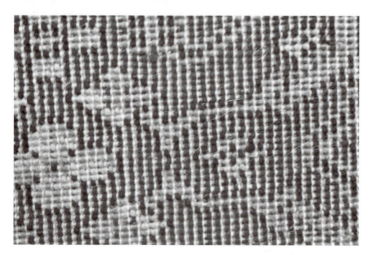

Figure 7-22. The Axminster pattern is woven through the back.

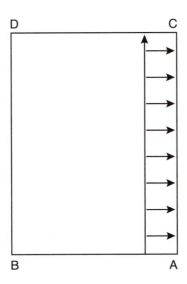

**Figure 7-23. Installing Axminster weave carpet.**
**Step 1: Power-stretch from corner A to corner C and hook the carpet.**
**Use straight knee kicks along wall AC and hook the carpet.**

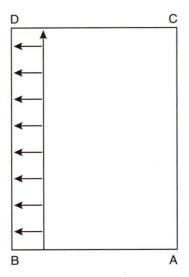

**Figure 7-24. Installing Axminster weave carpet.**
**Step 2: Power-stretch from corner B to corner D and hook the carpet.**
**Use straight knee kicks along wall BD and hook the carpet.**

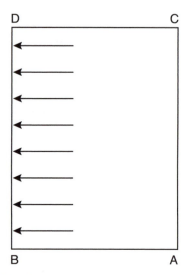

**Figure 7-25. Installing Axminster weave carpet.**
**Step 3: Power-stretch along wall AC and hook the carpet along wall BD.**

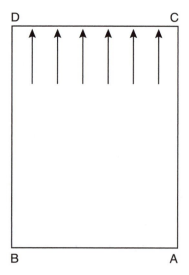

**Figure 7-26. Installing Axminster weave carpet.**
**Step 4: Power-stretch along wall BA and hook the carpet along wall DC.**

**Figure 7-27. Installing Axminster carpet.**
**Step 5: Use straight knee kicks and hook the carpet along wall BD.**

### Tufted Carpet Installation

Seaming and stretching tufted carpet is easier than with woven carpet. Non-loop pile fabrics do not ravel as easily, so seam sealing is only necessary along cut edges that must be seamed, or where the carpet meets a transition, such as at a family room/kitchen entry where the carpet butts up against a hard surface. Loop-pile carpets, however, must be sealed along all edges. Remember, *there is no such thing as an invisible seam.* A strip of *seaming tape* is centered under the two pieces of fabric to be joined. The tape has up to nine rows of hardened glue set on heavy paper (Figure 7-28). A *seaming iron* (Figure 7-29), with a bottom the same width as the tape, is heated electrically to melt the glue and spread it as the iron is moved along the length of the tape (Figure 7-30). Some irons use electronic waves instead of heat to melt the tape. Some irons have a Vshaped groove on the back end that channels hot glue between the two sheets of fabric, sealing the seam in one step. Pre-sealing the seams when using this type of iron is unnecessary.

The installer will pause every foot or so to fold the fabric edges down into the hot glue, pressing the edges together to form a closely butted seam and allowing the glue to set up, grab the backing, and harden. A weighted board is placed behind the installer to maintain pressure while the glue spreads and hardens. The installer must be careful not to overlap any portion of the carpet along the seam. Overlaps make the pile higher on one side of the seam than the other, creating a seam that is highly visible. The face yarn must also be kept from curling into the glue and sticking there. Once the glue cools, the two pieces of carpet are fused into one strong sheet of material.

**Figure 7-28. Carpet seaming tape.**

**Figure 7-29. Seaming iron.**

**Figure 7-30. Pressing the back of the carpet into the melted glue.**

Hot-melt seaming is fast and effective. Well-made seams are hardly noticeable (no one should promise you an invisible seam!) and hold up under repeated cleanings. Properly seamed areas wear as well as non-seamed areas, as long as the adhesive sticks to the backing and the seam tape does not split.

After seaming, the installers will stretch the carpet into place. Tufted carpet stretches in all directions and, like the other constructions, is installed in a predetermined sequence.

The installers begin by hooking the carpet onto the tackstrip pins at corner A (Figure 7-31). They put the power-stretcher pad in corner A, then power-stretch from A to C and hook the carpet onto the strip at corner C. Next, they place the power-stretcher pad at corner A and power-stretch from A to B and hook the carpet onto the tackstrip at corner B (Figure 7-32).

Then they use the knee kicker and bump it at a 15-degree angle to hook the carpet onto the strip along the entire wall A-C

(Figure 7-33). They follow the same pattern along wall A-B, kicking every few feet at a 15-degree angle and hooking the carpet onto the tackstrip (Figure 7-34).

Next, they put the stretcher pad in corner A and power-stretch at a 15-degree angle, moving the stretcher every few feet along wall B-D and hooking the carpet onto the strip from B to D. (Figure 7-35). Finally, they put the stretcher pad in corner B and power-stretch along the wall D-C, hooking the carpet onto the tackstrip as they move along (Figure 7-36). Then they trim the excess carpet with the edge trimmer and push the edge of the carpet into the gully between the tackstrip and wall with the stair tool or wide blade to finish the job.

Properly installed carpet is smooth around the room edges and tight in the center of the room. If you see your installer using only a knee kicker and then pull out an electric stapler to fasten the carpet around the room perimeters, throw the bum out! Your carpet will be looser in the center of the room, and will have "dimples" around the edges. Once the carpet gets a little walking on it, the carpet will probably wrinkle badly.

**Figure 7-31. Installing tufted carpet.**
**Step 1: Power-stretch from corner A to corner C and hook the carpet.**

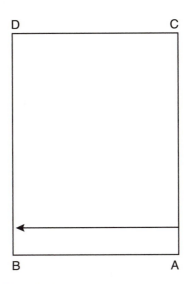

**Figure 7-32. Installing tufted carpet.**
**Step 2: Power-stretch from corner A to corner B and hook the carpet.**

**Figure 7-33. Installing tufted carpet.**
**Step 3: Knee-kick and hook along wall AC.**

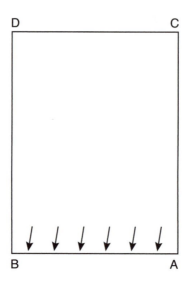

**Figure 7-34. Installing tufted carpet.**
**Step 4: Knee-kick at a 15-degree angle and hook along wall AB.**

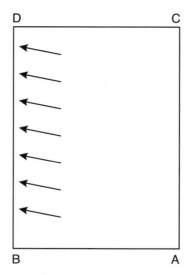

**Figure 7-35. Installing tufted carpet. Step 5: Power-stretch at a 15-degree angle and hook along wall BD.**

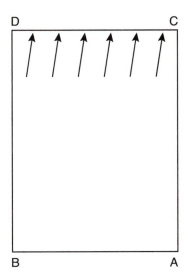

**Figure 7-36. Installing tufted carpet. Step 6: Power-stretch at a 15-degree angle and hook along wall DC.**

## ONE LAST REASON FOR PROFESSIONAL INSTALLATION

The previous section explaining installation should have convinced you that do-it-yourself installation is not a great idea. I have one more reason why you should hire a professional installer: *the carpet warranty.*

All first-quality carpet comes with a one-year unconditional warranty against defects in manufacturing. However, many mills will not cover carpet that is installed by a do-it-yourselfer. Here's why. Professionals know that they cannot install carpet that has a defect, obvious or not, because mills do not like to take back carpet that has been installed. As professionals, they can spot some defects before the carpet is even unrolled. Once they unroll the carpet, they'll inspect it before the first cut. They could find different problems. They'll stop the installation if they need to and call the retailer or factory before going further.

If you do it yourself (D-I-Y), you probably wouldn't recognize many defects. You could install the whole job before you realize you have to make a claim. By then the mill's claim department is thinking, "Is this a case of buyer's remorse?" So, be warned! You could get stuck with a lot of defective carpet if you D-I-Y. I can tell you as a Certified Flooring Inspector with 40 years in the business, I have never looked at a D-I-Y claim because the mills will not honor them!

But take heart. You do have other choices. You can hire your own freelance installer. Or you can use the workroom offered by the retailer or designer.

Hiring the right independent installer will take some work. Do the same legwork you would do if you were hiring a contractor for a remodel. Ask around. Check references. Look at jobs they have completed. Check out their license and insurance—very important! Are they Certified Flooring Installers? You may save money and get a great job by hiring your own crew, but do you want to act as your own contractor? Keep in mind, some independents work on a shoestring and live from job to job. They can't afford any problems. If you have a complaint about materials or workmanship, some freelancers couldn't handle the problem. If they can not afford the delay to their cash flow, they may just "disappear."

All carpet retailers and decorators offer in-house carpet installation as part of their "total package" philosophy. Most people assume that a dealer's installers will do a top-notch job. That happens most of the time, but not always. Larger stores keep several crews busy; realistically, quality can vary from one crew to another. If a crew is newly hired, the retailer may not have seen any of their previous work. Most installers are subcontractors, not store employees.

As a rule, in-house installers are excellent. A retailer could not afford to keep a bad installer around for long. Although installation is technically the installer's responsibility, the dealer has a large stake—money and reputation—in how well the job is done. So do you. Retailers know you'll be calling them, not the installer, if there are installation problems.

So do your homework. Find out which crew will do your installation. How long have they worked with your retailer? What is their work history? How long have they installed carpet? Are they Certified Flooring Installers?

Whichever alternative you decide is right for you—independents or in-house—once the carpet is installed and furniture is placed in the rooms, you will probably enjoy the finished job more because you understand both the carpet you bought and how it was installed.

# 8

# CARPET MAINTENANCE

What can you do to keep your beautiful and expensive carpet looking showroom new? Plan to care for your carpet in a number of ways involving both short- and long-term maintenance. In the short term, regular vacuuming and spotting works wonders to keep the carpet looking good. Over the long term, plan on (and budget for) regular professional cleaning to maintain your investment. Most carpet warranties require periodic *professional* cleanings to keep the warranty in effect. You must show the carpet cleaning receipts if you file a claim. Some warranties also specify the *type* of cleaning needed to keep the warranty in effect.

## VACUUM CLEANERS

Regular vacuuming is probably the single most helpful thing a person can do to maintain a carpet's appearance. How often to vacuum depends on traffic, lifestyle, and where you live. The more people and pets living in a home means more vacuuming. If you live in a large city with a lot of dust and soot, you'll vacuum more. Likewise, if you live near a beach or in dry, dusty areas, you'll vacuum more.

It is recommended that under average household conditions (four people, one pet), a carpet should be vacuumed at least twice a week—once lightly, once thoroughly. A light vacuuming means two to three forward and back overlapping passes of the machine in each of the high-traffic areas, with one pass in the low traffic areas.

Heavy vacuuming means at least six back and forth overlapping passes of the machine in the high usage areas, one to two in the other areas. It is a lot of work, but your carpet will thank you for it by looking new longer. Your pocketbook will thank you because the carpet will need fewer professional cleanings. Remember that grit and sand rubbing at the base of the fibers is what causes a carpet to get dull and worn looking.

I'm often asked if a carpet can be vacuumed too much. Today's synthetic fabrics are made to be vacuumed. Many maintain their appearance only by vacuuming. Normally, most vacuums work well with most kinds of fabrics, but some heavy duty machines teamed with delicate fibers such as wool or soft, fine nylon can cause problems. Strong motors and stiff brushes can distort cut-pile patterns and make Berber-type looped fabrics look fuzzy or stringy. A vacuum brush that is soft to medium in stiffness is the safest for most carpets. If your vacuum has adjustable brushes, it is also better to set the brushes higher rather than lower. You should feel little resistance against the carpet when you vacuum. Some manufacturers suggest that it is better for the brushes to barely touch the pile. This prevents you from beating the carpet to death.

There are a lot of variables to selecting the "right" vacuum. You can't buy a vacuum based on price alone. How do you find a vacuum that works well with your carpet? The independent Carpet and Rug Institute tests all types of vacuums. The CRI does not accept money from vacuum manufacturers. Their only aim is to independently help you find the correct vacuum for your needs. You can go to their home page at www.carpet-rug.org. Then click on Residential Customers, then Cleaning and Maintenance, then Seal of Approval Products, and select Vacuums. The Institute has a long list of approved, efficient machines with links to the manufacturers' websites. In general, the Institute has found that upright vacuums outperform tank-type or canisters, even when the tanks have a separate power-driven beater-bar attachment called a *power head.*

The fact is that an upright agitates the pile yarns better and creates a more efficient partial vacuum inside the suction chamber. Uprights, which fill from the top, are the most efficient and blow less dust around than bottom-filling models.

One can argue the fine points between uprights and canisters. The main thing is to *use the machine you have.* It won't help the carpet to keep the vacuum in the closet!

Vacuum maintenance is also very important. Any machine needs attention occasionally, and a vacuum cleaner is no exception. A weak vacuum cannot pick up dirt and lint. A clean vacuum bag (or an empty tank with "bagless" machines) does wonders to increase suction and efficiency. A full bag is probably the most common reason a machine works improperly. Bags fill up more quickly than people realize, so keep an eye on them. Replace the bag when it is half full.

Worn out beater-bar brushes do not provide the correct agitation to loosen soil from the yarn and lift it from the carpet backing. Look at the brushes occasionally and see if they are frayed or worn down. Often string or pet hair wraps around the brushes and keeps them from working properly. Cut away any foreign material and keep the brushes clean. If the brushes look stubbly, replace them with new ones. Remember, the brushes must at least touch the carpet slightly to remove the dirt. Also, be aware that some brushes contain bristles that are very stiff. A stiff bristled brush used on a softer fabric will make the yarns untwist. The carpet will look new against the wall but will look old where it is vacuumed improperly. (Figure 8-1.)

Check the belt now and then. I check the vacuum during each carpet inspection I conduct. You'd be surprised at how many people think their vacuum works well until I check the belt and find it is broken. Replace the belt if it's cracked or stretched out. A broken belt wastes your vacuuming energy because you are pushing the vacuum but it's not doing anything but making noise! And when a belt breaks during use, the hot rubber can put a black streak on the carpet that may not come out.

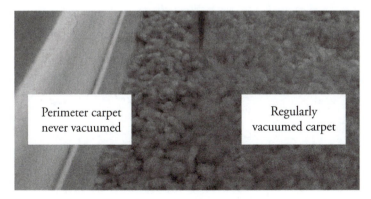

Perimeter carpet
never vacuumed

Regularly
vacuumed carpet

**Figure 8-1. Carpet pile badly fuzzed by stiff vacuum brushes set too low.**

## SPOT REMOVERS

Everyone gets a spot on their carpet occasionally, and many remedies, purchased and homemade, are available. Choosing the right spotter depends on the type of foreign matter spilled on the carpet fiber. Most spills in the home are divided into two groups—water-based spills and oil-based spills. Water-based spills include milk, juices, and carbonated beverages. Oil-based spills include cooking oils, butter, car oil, and tar, to name a few.

Whatever you use as a spotter, avoid foamy, soap-based commercial products. If you gently shake the container and the solution gets sudsy, look for a different product. These cleaners are supposed to remove all types of spots, but often they only bury the original contaminant under a layer of suds (Figure 8-2). Optical brighteners in the foam make it appear that the spot is gone. Then the soap film soon begins to attract dirt because soap is what? A dirt magnet! Then the spot slowly reappears.

Rinsing with clear water would normally reduce or eliminate the resoiling problem, but the foam is really hard to remove, even by a professional. To make matters worse, some of these cleaners can slowly bleach the color out of the carpet. Spot-testing first is not always a help, because the discoloring happens so slowly that it may not be noticeable for days or even weeks. If the color is not actually bleached, optical brighteners literally cover up the carpet dye and leave a light area. These brighteners attach themselves permanently to the carpet fibers and can't be removed.

**Figure 8-2. Soap residue in carpet pile.**

Fortunately, the Carpet and Rug Institute has also tested commercially available carpet spotting solutions and listed the safe ones on its website. Search as you did for vacuums. You will find Spot Cleaners listed under Seal of Approval Products.

You also have the compound needed to remove water-based spots right in your tap—that's right, water! Plain water usually removes water-based spots such as soda, milk, and juice. The synthetic stain-resistant fibers will release most colors. It's the sugar that causes spots to reappear after you've cleaned up the obvious spill. Sugar is sticky and attracts dirt. So you have to safely clean the sugar out of the carpet fiber.

## PROPER SPOT CLEANING

First blot up the excess spill with a terrycloth towel. Then use a trigger-type sprayer to apply warm water after the first blotting. How much water depends on the size of the spill and the thickness of the carpet. Do not soak the fabric. Try to work from the outside of the spill towards its center to keep the spot from getting bigger. *Do not rub!*

Spray enough water so that the sugars dissolve. Blot again and feel the fabric. If it still feels sticky, repeat the above steps several times. Remember: *blot, don't rub*. Rubbing untwists the yarn. The pile will look fuzzy when it dries. Rubbing also pulls individual fibers from the carpet backing. The area you've spot cleaned will look like it's growing a beard.

If a water-based spill dries before you have a chance to remove it, you'll have to rewet it so that the sugars begin to dissolve. Use a trigger sprayer and mist warm water onto the sticky spot until it is just moistened. Use an old toothbrush to gently tamp the water into the spot. You can also brush *gently* in one direction being careful not to distort the yarns. Work in the water and loosen any particles.

You may have to add a *few* drops of clear (not cloudy) liquid dish detergent to the water. This helps loosen and remove foreign particles such as orange rind or mud. If you use any detergent, you must spray the fabric thoroughly with clear water after the spot is removed. Blot again with terrycloth towels and feel the fabric. If it still feels soapy slick, keep spraying on warm clear water and blotting until the area feels clean. Otherwise, the soap residue will attract dirt and the spot will come back. If the cleaned area seems too wet, place several layers of toweling over the spot. Then put a weight, such as a pot filled with water, over the affected area. The towels will pull out the excess moisture. You'll have the added benefit of any remaining spill soaking up into the toweling, too.

If you still can't get the spill out, go to the www.carpet-rug.org website. Look for their Spot Solver link. There you will find a list of every conceivable thing that can possibly spot your carpet and ways to remove them. I would avoid commercial spot removers, if possible.

Oily stains can only be removed by solvents that dissolve the foreign substance from the carpet yarn. You can find familiar names such as Energine, Thuro, and Goddard's dry-cleaning fluids. Dry cleaning fluids evaporate without leaving a ring and do not need rinsing. Besides oils and butter, they remove tar, grease, and small amounts of candle wax. But use these products carefully and sparingly. *They can eat away the latex bond between the carpet backing, causing the yarn to fall out!*

You should only apply these fluids to your terrycloth towel, *never* directly to the carpet. Then *gently* blot the spot towards its center to avoid spreading it. You can use a soft toothbrush to loosen particles of tar or wax. You may have to repeat the application. If you've spilled more than a few drops of oil to the carpet and it's soaked down towards the backing, call a professional cleaner for help. Don't ruin your carpet. Never use gasoline, paint removers, or any highly flammable or toxic solvents in your home or on your carpet.

## ODORS

Invisible odors are as much an annoyance as stains. But they are caused by microorganisms living somewhere in the carpet or pad and signal a potential health hazard. Carpet fresheners and deodorizers do not help much, no matter how heavily they are advertised. Dumping perfumed baking soda on a smelly carpet won't remove the odor-causing bacteria or fungus. Milk, urine, water, or any number of substances are food for these organisms.

Deodorizers which are sprayed or sprinkled simply cover up the odors but do not attack the source. The foreign substance must be removed to get rid of the odor-causing bacteria. Sometimes, as with severe mildew or saturation by urine, replacement of the carpet and pad is the only sure cure. On occasion, pets will soak a favorite area of the carpet so much that the underlying floor is also affected. Then the carpet must be taken up, the pad replaced, and the floor cleaned and sealed to keep any remaining odor locked in.

Packaged fresheners cannot cure these problems. The best protection is prevention. Then have your spotting kit ready to go. And have your carpets cleaned on a regular basis. A Certified cleaning professional has chemicals in his/her arsenal which completely neutralize (as opposed to masking) the offending odor. A good cleaner knows how to inject the chemical into the pad if necessary.

There are carpet cushions available that protect against spills and pet stains. These pads have anti-microbial treatments and a plastic top sheet to aide clean-up and prevent odors.

## DO-IT-YOURSELF CLEANING

Many people like to clean their own carpets, especially between professional cleanings. It is easy to rent a variety of cleaning equipment. You can find rental equipment at supermarkets and equipment rental stores. Keep in mind that carpet cleaning is a lot of work and the results may be disappointing. Let's look at the three most popular methods used: shampooing, dry cleaning, and steam cleaning.

### Shampooing

*Rotary shampooing* is the oldest method for cleaning carpets. It is what most people think of when they hear "carpet cleaning." You must thoroughly vacuum your carpet first to remove as much grit and dust as possible. A shampoo machine uses one or two flat, rotating brushes to work a shampoo solution into the carpet pile. There is no vacuum or extraction system to pull out any shampoo or dirt. The mechanical action of the brushes combines with the shampoo to lift the dirt from the yarn and break any oil film. After the carpet dries, the shampoo turns to a powder which is vacuumed up along with any remaining soil.

While shampooing leaves the carpet looking clean, much of the dirt has actually been driven to the carpet backing and covered with a layer of detergent film. Because there is no way to rinse and extract the shampoo and dirt, a lot of it stays in the carpet pile. This residue leads to rapid resoiling. Many people think that because a carpet gets dirty so quickly after shampooing, it must be better to wait as long as possible to clean it the first time. That is why many people use a wet vac to remove as much solution as possible. A better alternative is, after shampooing, to rinse and extract the fabric using a "steam cleaner." A combination of shampoo and extraction is the best method for cleaning heavily soiled carpeting.

Shampooing creates two more risks. It is easy to over-wet the carpet, causing shrinking or delamination (the backing comes off). Also, the scrubbing action of the brushes can distort some cut-pile fabrics, untwisting the face yarns and making the carpet look fuzzy. Non-wool loop carpets hold up to shampooing better.

## Dry Cleaning

When *dry cleaning*, an absorbent powder impregnated with water and cleaning solvents is sprinkled onto the carpet. The Host System is widely available through rental equipment stores. A machine uses opposing rotary brushes to work the powder into the pile. The solvent dissolves oils. The water frees soils trapped in the yarn. The powder acts as sponges and absorbs the soil. The powder and soil are then vacuumed up. In high-traffic areas with heavy soil, a traffic lane cleaner is misted on before the powder is applied. This chemical helps loosen soil, dissolve oil/grease, and increase the overall effectiveness of the absorbent powder.

Dry cleaning has its good points. The rotary machine acts as a pile lifter, pulling apart entangled face yarns and restoring the carpet's appearance. The equipment is easy to use, and it is impossible to over-wet the fabric. The carpet can be walked on right away because it is not wet. Dry cleaning is also good for touching up high-traffic areas between professional cleanings. It leaves behind very little residue when done correctly. You *must* use an upright vacuum in good condition to remove all the powder and soil. Dry cleaning works best on lightly to moderately soiled carpet that is not heavily spotted.

The dry method has a few drawbacks to consider. The brushes can cause tip flair and distortion, especially on some high profile, soft fabrics. The brush bristles range from soft to stiff. You may not have a choice of brushes if you rent the equipment. Test-clean a small area to make sure that the brushes are right for your carpet.

Also, the powder is hard to remove from long heavy piles. You must thoroughly vacuum, preferably from two directions, to remove as much powder as possible.

## "Steam" Cleaning

"Steam" cleaning is a misleading name for the most effective cleaning method. Actually, no steam is used to clean the carpet. Hot water and a cleaning solution are mixed in a tank on the portable cleaning machine. The solution is pressure pumped down a hose and through a small triangular-shaped jet at the carpet end of the cleaning wand onto the carpet. As the wand is dragged towards you, this warm solution (the water loses a lot of heat traveling through the hose) dissolves dirt from the carpet pile and puts it into a suspension. A vacuum behind the pressure jet sucks out the water and soil almost immediately, leaving a damp fabric. The dirty water goes into a holding tank next to the hot water tank. *Hot-water extraction* is a longer but more accurate term for this system.

Hot-water extraction has several advantages over the other cleaning methods. It removes more soil and more types of soil than shampooing or absorbent powder. Because it uses no brushes, there is virtually no chance for pile distortion. The concentrated cleaning solution is diluted with the hot water so residue buildup and resoiling are kept to a minimum.

The system has one big disadvantage for the beginning carpet cleaner. Repeated cleaning of a heavily soiled area can cause overwetting and damage: mildew, delamination, subfloor warping, etc.

You should also know that the chemicals sold with rental machines are not "professional strength." They are watered down so they are "goof-proof." This means heavily soiled areas are more difficult to clean completely than if a professional cleans them. Also, the vacuum suction and the water pressure from the jet are not very strong. Repeatedly cleaning a problem area will not make a cleaner carpet, only a wetter one. More is not better. If a dirty area doesn't clean up after two or three tries, give up. Carpet cleaning is one of the harder things you can do yourself. For all the effort, the results can't compare to a thorough professional cleaning.

## PROFESSIONAL CLEANING

Most carpet warranties today *require* a cleaning every 12 to 24 months in order to keep the warranty in effect. This is no different from a car manufacturer's requiring you to change the oil every so many miles or so many months. Some warranties specify the type of cleaning, too. Most mills require *professional* hot-water extraction cleaning. If you put in a claim, you must show your cleaning receipt.

Professional cleaners will have chemicals and equipment that are not available to the average homeowner. They will also have specialized training and a lot of experience dealing with different types of soiled carpeting. And the results are usually a lot better than doing it yourself. Sure, there are a lot of horror stories about this cleaner who soaked a carpet so badly that it was wet for three days, or that cleaner who left so much residue in the carpet that it was dirty again in three weeks. But these stories are like the evening news. You only hear about the bad stuff. The good stuff seldom makes the news. Carpet cleaners are like everyone else. Most are good. Some are truly excellent at their craft. Using a professional cleaner to help maintain your expensive carpeting is just plain smart.

Take a long look at your carpet when you think about cleaning it. Check the color. Does it look dull or gray? Look at the face pile. Are the tufts stuck together? Is soil visible? Is the nap badly crushed? Are there spots you couldn't get out? Professional cleaning should take care of all these problems.

There are reasons why the mills want their carpets cleaned on a regular basis. Cleaning extends the life of the carpet. Light colors or high-traffic areas need regular attention. You should not wait until the traffic areas are so dirty that they look like a path through the woods. Soil and spots are harder to remove once they've been in the fabric a long time. And spots that would have come out fairly easily when relatively fresh-set are sometimes impossible to remove after several months have passed. So don't wait—call your carpet cleaner as needed to keep your carpet looking good for the longest possible time.

### Locating a Professional Cleaner

You can begin your search by going to the Institute of Inspection Cleaning and Restoration Certification. The name is a mouthful, but this is the oldest organization that trains and certifies carpet cleaners and flooring inspectors. I am certified in many areas through this organization. The training and testing is extensive. Once certified, members must take continuing-education courses offered around the country to maintain their certification. It is time consuming and expensive. Only professionals serious about their work bother to pass these tests and keep their certifications updated.

The IICRC maintains an up-to-date database of Certified Carpet Cleaners. You can search by zip code to find someone in your area. I can promise you that cleaners who advertise to clean your carpet for $5 per room will not show up on this list! Certified Carpet Cleaners must be competitively priced. But expect to pay for all the time, effort, and expense your cleaner took to reach his/her level of expertise.

If you live in a large metropolitan area you'll probably see several names on the Certified Carpet Cleaners list. Some names will be owner/operators. They own the company and do the work. Some will be nationally known cleaning franchises. Jot them down. Then ask everyone you know if they have used anyone on your list and ask for their recommendations. The search will be the same as if you were looking for a doctor or dentist. Sooner or later, a few names will top your list. Then call for more information. Ask a lot of questions. Make it sound like you really know the carpet cleaning business.

- What method of cleaning is used? (Almost any type of properly running truck-mounted hot-water extraction system is generally accepted by the mills.)
- Is each employee certified? (A company can be certified. It does not follow that each *employee* is certified.)
- Certified Carpet Cleaners are required to deep-vacuum before cleaning. Is this included in the price?
- Is furniture-moving part of the price? (Most cleaners include furniture moving in the price. Some give discounts if you move the smaller pieces out.)
- Is pre-spotting included in the estimate? (It usually is.)
- What type of cleaning agents are used? (Generally, soapless pre-sprays for traffic lanes are preferred. Emulsifiers are best for overall cleaning. Special spotters are used for blood, grease, rust, and chewing gum. Green and hypo-allergenic [non-perfumed] agents are available.)

If the person sounds intelligent, confident, and educated and has good customer skills, you may have found your cleaner.

Be prepared with your room measurements. Then ask the *big* question: *How much do you charge?* Most really good cleaners will fall into a fairly narrow price range—from moderately expensive to expensive. The most expensive in town won't necessarily do a better job than someone charging a little less. But expect to spend some money. You do get what you pay for. After checking with a few places on your list, you'll get a good idea of an average price. Most legitimate carpet cleaners charge by the square foot, not by the room. If the total price seems reasonable and you liked the recommendations from others, make an appointment and get the carpet cleaned.

It should go without saying that if something seems too good to be true, it probably is. This true story of the homeowner who saw a flyer advertising any room steam-cleaned for $4.95 (minimum three rooms) is typical. "What a deal," thought the individual. "I can get the living room, dining room, and family room cleaned for less than 15 bucks." So he booked an appointment and a "technician" came out to clean the carpet.

The portable machine he used was loud and not much bigger than the one for rent in the supermarket. It took a long time to clean the three rooms.

After the work was finished, the homeowner was handed a bill for $89.85! "Why is the bill so high? What happened to the $14.85?", asked the man. The technician calmly explained, "The steam cleaning was $14.85, all right. But the carpet was so dirty that I had to use a special conditioner which is $25 per gallon. And I had to use one gallon in each room. That makes the total $89.85."

After a lot of arguing, the consumer finally paid the bill, knowing it wouldn't happen again. The moral of the story is very simple: don't jump at bargain carpet cleaning without carefully checking it out.

## Professional Cleaning Methods

Professional cleaners use four methods to clean residential carpeting. They seem similar to the methods discussed earlier in the do-it-yourself cleaning section. But the equipment and chemicals professionals use are so much more efficient and thorough than rental equipment that there is just no comparison. Plus, a professional brings specialized training and an understanding of your expensive carpeting. Certified Carpet Cleaners often perform a walk-through, or "audit," of your carpet before they begin the work. They will check for weak seams, look for unusual stains, evaluate the wear patterns in the various rooms, possibly check your vacuum, and generally evaluate the overall installation.

Professional cleaners know you clean your carpets to keep them looking good and to maintain their warranties. They know that deep-cleaning carpets also protects your health. Carpet is actually a huge filter in your home. It traps not only dirt, but allergens like pet dander and pollen. It also holds dust mites. Professional cleaners know how to remove these contaminants.

**Shampoo.** As explained earlier, shampooing a carpet leaves a residue in the fibers. However, professional shampooing is often used when a carpet is too dirty for cleaning by hot-water extraction alone. A cleaning solution is dispensed from a tank to the cleaning brushes. The brushes are available with different bristle stiffnesses for different carpet textures and are usually 15 inches in diameter. The brush scrubs the solution into the carpet pile.

The shampoo lifts the dirt off the fibers and holds it in suspension. The best long-term results are achieved when shampooing is used with a rinse-and-extract system to flush out the suspended soil and shampoo residue. The operator must take care not to over-wet the carpet or allow cut-pile fabrics to fuzz.

**Dry Foam.** The dry-foam system uses rotating brushes to apply a drier type of shampoo to the carpet pile. It uses a wet vacuum pickup to remove water and dirt. The carpet dries more quickly because less water is used in the process. It leaves less residue than ordinary shampooing, and the fuzzing of cut pile fabrics is reduced. The carpet should still be rinsed and extracted for best long-term results.

**Dry Clean.** Dry-powder cleaning has been around for decades. The basic way the system works hasn't changed much over the years. Main walkways are first treated with a traffic lane cleaner to loosen any heavy soil. A powder, either chemical or natural, is brushed or otherwise worked into the carpet face yarns. The powder granules absorb grit, dirt, and oils.

After a short time, the powder and the soils adhered to it are vacuumed up and the carpet is ready for immediate use. Dry cleaning leaves little residue to retract soil. It works best on lightly soiled fabrics. Some people use it between hot-water extraction cleanings. This system works best for your convenience and comfort.

**Hot-Water Extraction.** Hot water extraction, or "steam" cleaning, is probably the best overall system used by professionals today. As I said earlier, most major carpet producers require regular extraction cleaning if you want to keep your carpet warranties in effect.

Either a portable or truck-mounted system is used. Portable equipment is wheeled. The better portable machines are many times more powerful than rental units, even though they look similar. The professional units have more powerful water pumps for a stronger spray, larger vacuum motors for more suction, and heating units inside the water tanks. Higher water temperatures make the cleaning chemicals work better. Some approach the power of smaller truck-mounted machines. Portable machines are easy to carry on and off the job. They are also easier to set up and easier to handle than truck-mounted systems. Portable machines are especially good for multi-unit high-rise work and are also preferable for condos when the parking lot is far away.

However, a truck-mounted hot-water extraction system—from now on called a steam cleaner for simplicity—is still more powerful. It is just right for stand-alone residential carpet cleaning. The operator pulls up to the front door, unwinds the hot water and vacuum hoses to the farthest point to be cleaned, attaches the hoses to the machine in the back of the van, and is ready to begin cleaning. These machines make their own hot water and usually pump the dirty water into your home's sewage system. The water temperature and pressure can be dialed up or dialed down, according to the carpet type and soil level.

Most homeowners prefer truck-mounted steam cleaning for several reasons. The machine stays outside so there is no chance that a heavy machine will bump into furniture or walls. The truck mounts have thermostats to control the water temperature so that each type of carpet fiber, such as wool or nylon, is properly treated. Water pressure is also regulated. Normal pressure is 400 to 500 pounds per square inch. This means very little water volume is needed to wash or rinse the fabric.

Most of these machines have a cleaning solution shut-off. The cleaning is followed by a hot-water rinse. This final rinse is very important because it removes all the cleaning chemicals as well as any remaining soil. The carpet literally feels squeaky clean, with no slick soapy feel.

The vacuums in these units are so strong that over 90 percent of the water (and the suspended soils) is removed during cleaning. Some cleaners use a drying agent in the rinse water and high-speed carpet fans to increase drying times. When carpets dry quickly, there is less chance that spots will wick up and reappear.

The carpet will stay clean just as long as when it was new. There is no dirt-attracting residue in the pile to cause rapid resoiling. When carpets are cleaned this way, the old wives' tale about carpets getting dirtier right after cleaning is finally laid to rest. In fact, side by side cleanings comparing truck-mount systems to other systems always show the truck mounts coming out on top.

# 9

# CARPET: CHARACTERISTICS & DEFECTS

So often, a person makes a major purchase, such as carpeting, only to be unpleasantly surprised by the product's performance. This section explains common characteristics and typical defects that are common to all carpets in all price ranges. The carpet industry has its own set of tolerances, variations, and specifications for the appearance and performance of its products. Your expectations might not be the same as those of the industry. Some things that might appear as a defect to you are considered normal by the industry.

Some of these characteristics are mentioned in the warranty. But how many people read the "fine print"? And how many people understand the fine print, anyway? As a long time flooring inspector, I can tell you that many misunderstandings could be avoided if more people knew exactly what to expect from their carpets, both as newly installed and after a few years in a home. Unfortunately, these things are seldom mentioned when the carpet is sold. The good news is, for first-quality carpets, all manufacturing defects are covered by a one-year warranty that covers correction or replacement (but usually not labor). And here's a word to the wise: Since you never know what will happen to your carpet, *always* put away some leftover carpet to save for repairs. Burns and tears are easy to repair *if* fabric is available. Don't let the installers take all the scrap.

This may seem like a long list of potential problems. You may even say to yourself, "Gee, if so many things can go wrong with carpet, maybe I should buy another type of flooring." Keep in mind that the carpet industry makes millions of square yards of broadloom each year.

Claims affect 2 to 4 percent of sales. So the total amount of carpet involved in claims is very small. The chance that something will affect your carpet is low. Besides, as a flooring inspector, I can tell you that *every* type of flooring has its own problems.

## SHEDDING

*Shedding* is common to all new carpet, especially cut-pile carpet. Some fuzz is produced by the shearing process and remains in the pile. Both continuous filament and staple yarns shed fuzz and fluff when new. You must vacuum out this excess fiber. It takes anywhere from two weeks to three months to remove most of the fuzz. It may appear that a lot of fiber is disappearing into the vacuum bag, but compared to the overall weight of the carpet face yarn, it isn't much at all.

One advantage of carpet made with continuous filament yarn is that once the initial fuzz is gone, the fabric stops shedding entirely. Staple yarns always shed, at least a little. Cheaper plush carpets sometimes are made with short staple-spun yarns that can shed a lot throughout the life of the carpet. Sometimes shedding is not normal. If the filaments that are spun together to form a tuft are not properly locked into the primary backing by the latex glue, filament slippage results. If you've had your cut pile carpet for more than a few months and the vacuum bag fills after each use, you may have a problem. Likewise, if you have a Berber or other loop-style carpet and you see the loops getting fuzzy, call your retailer.

One note: Wool loop-pile carpets are sensitive to vacuuming. If the vacuum brushes are set too low, or the brushes are too stiff, the vacuum will pull wool fibers from the backing even if the carpet is made properly. This type of fuzzing is considered to be maintenance related, not manufacturing related.

## PILLING

*Pilling* (Figure 9-1) is a condition directly related to shedding. Sometimes the vacuum cleaner cannot keep up with the amount of fluff coming from the pile. The brushes are unable to completely pull the fuzz from the carpet pile. The fluff collects on the surface of the carpet. With walking, the fuzz rolls up into little balls called pills. Soon the carpet looks like an old sweater.

If the vacuum isn't working properly to remove shedding, your carpet will pill. Check to make sure the belt is on correctly. Is the vacuum bag more than half full? Empty it. Is the brush set at the right height? Proper height adjustment allows the brushes to remove the fuzz without overly beating the pile.

If the vacuum is working efficiently and the carpet is pilling, call your retailer. He may need to call for a carpet inspector to determine the cause of the pilling. Sometimes an unused piece of scrap can be sent to a testing laboratory to see if it's made correctly.

If the carpet is okay, the pills can be removed by shearing the carpet pile. Pilling usually affects only new carpet. Once sheared, the condition normally does not return.

**Figure 9-1. Fuzzed and pilled carpet pile.**

## SHADING

*Shading* is an apparent color difference between areas of the same carpet. It is a common complaint with cut pile carpets. The industry considers it a "normal characteristic of cut pile fabrics." Shading ranges in intensity from slight to severe. It is caused by the face yarns changing the direction of their lay. Footprints and vacuum wheel marks are two type of shading, caused when the yarns are crushed down (Figure 9-2).

You also sometimes see shading along a seam. One side looks lighter than the other when you enter a room. Then when you walk to the other end of the room and look back, it appears that the lighter/darker sides have changed places; what looked lighter from one end now looks darker and what looked darker now looks lighter. This happens when the rolled up carpet, before installation, shifts and distorts the face yarns. It isn't noticeable until the roll is cut and seamed. Then the face yarns run in two directions along the seam, making an apparent color difference. Light is reflected from the yarn sides and yarn tips at different rates, making light and dark areas. Shading along a seam is corrected by hand steaming the pile on both sides of the seam in the same direction. The machine used is similar to a wall paper steamer. It resets the pile distortion so that the pile on each side of the seam goes the same way, removing the shading. This is effective only with wool or nylon face piles.

**Figure 9-2. Shading in cut pile carpeting.**

Shading is considered normal for all cut pile fabrics because the pile does not always lay in one direction. Because shading is a characteristic of a certain type of fabric, mills rarely consider it to be a legitimate complaint.

The following is a shading disclaimer from a mill specializing in high end woven carpets:

> Shading, also referred to as watermarking, roll crush, or reverse pile, can occur on all cut pile materials, which is an inherent effect on the product regardless of fiber or quality. The cause is unknown, and the rate of incidence is unpredictable despite extreme industry research.

Further, there is no method to make it occur or likewise a method of prevention, and therefore is not considered to be a manufacturing defect. As a result, claims will not be considered for this condition. Normal foot traffic and frequent, thorough vacuuming should improve the condition.

Shading does not happen with all cut pile carpets. The longer, softer naps tend to show more footprints. People have been known to get so upset by their carpet's showing footprints and vacuum marks that they have ripped up new carpet, thrown it out, and replaced it with another texture that doesn't show marks! Textured Saxonys are sometimes called "trackless" carpets because they show less shading. They tend to be shorter and nubbier than other Saxonys or plushes. Just know that if you choose some variation of a cut pile carpet, you will probably have some degree of shading.

## PILE REVERSAL

Shading is seen all over a cut pile carpet. *Pile reversal or reverse pile* (Figure 9-3) is an extreme form of shading with the pile yarns laying on their sides, causing the carpet to look darker in the affected areas. You see it mostly in high-traffic areas (think hallways) or at pivot points (like doorways). Pile reversal is similar to crushed-velvet furniture fabrics, with light and dark shades.

Figure 9-3. Traffic lane pile reversal.

Some people think shading and pile reversal are ugly because the color is uneven. Others consider it the mark of a fine quality carpet. Oriental rugs often have shading or pile reversal. But the rugs' ornate patterns tend to make these conditions less noticeable. At any rate, mills will not replace a carpet for pile reversal because they know the replacement will probably reverse, too.

## Pooling

*Pooling* or *watermarking* is the most severe form of pile reversal (Figure 9-4), seen mostly in velvet plushes. The face yarns reverse direction and sometimes lay almost flat in an irregular circle that can reach several feet across. The areas look so dark that it looks like someone poured a bucket of water onto the carpet, hence the name "watermark." Pooling can happen in traffic lanes. I have also seen it appear under furniture. No one can explain exactly why some plushes pool and others don't. But it is not considered a defect, and mills won't replace your carpet if it watermarks. There is no method to permanently correct pooling, since the face yarns can always change direction again.

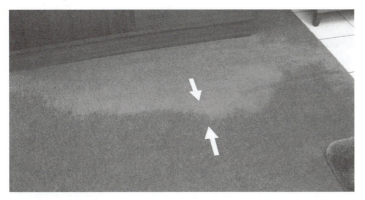

**Figure 9-4. Pooling.**

## Roll Crush

*Roll crush* (sometimes called *roll crush marks)* is a type of pile reversal found only on new carpet, whether cut pile or loop pile. It is characterized by a series of widthwise lines or bands running across the roll. (Figure 9-5). The crush marks are areas of the pile that are crushed flat and have reversed direction while the rest of the carpet pile is standing up. Carpet rolls are 100 feet to 120 feet in length and are very heavy. When rolls are warehoused, they are often stacked on top of each other for a period of time. This extreme weight crushes the bottom rolls. The crush marks form in the flattened sections of the rolls.

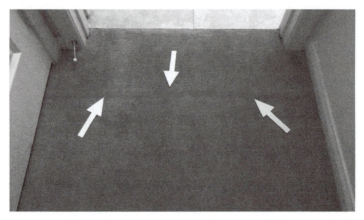

**Figure 9-5. Crush mark.**

When the carpet is unrolled, it looks like a football field. The distance between the marks depends on the distance from the center of the roll. Inner roll crush marks are 1 to 2 feet apart. Those farther from the core might be 2 to 5 feet apart. The appearance varies widely from a single crease to overall distortion or a wrinkled appearance.

Unlike other types of pile reversal, roll crush sometimes goes away by itself in a few weeks just from vacuuming and walking, especially if the condition is slight and humidity is high. If it doesn't go away, the marks can be easily and permanently removed as long as the pile is wool or nylon. Just as ironing a blouse with a steam iron removes wrinkles, applying steam to the carpet relaxes the fibers. When steamed and gently brushed, the pile returns to its normal direction and the streaks disappear. Your retailer can send a professional to your home to steam the carpet.

Ideally, a dry steam should be used, from a machine like a Jiffy Steamer or a wallpaper remover. These machines boil water in a self-contained tank. The steam goes through a plastic hose and out through a flat nozzle with several holes. These steamers are also used to remove wrinkles from clothing and draperies. They are safe for all fabrics.

Because the carpet remains dry, it can be used almost immediately after service.

If dry steamers are not available, steam cleaning with very hot water and no cleaning solution will also remove the marks. The wet pile is brushed or raked to blend the pile and remove the crush marks.

## CRUSHING/MATTING

Crushing and matting are two common problems that are easy to confuse. *Crushing* is the flattening down of face yarns through normal use, especially with cut pile carpets. Carpeted traffic areas like hallways typically show crushing. An area directly in front of furniture, such as a chair facing the TV, will crush. When the carpet is vacuumed, the pile should stand up again. It is normal for the *tip* of the tuft to open. This is called *blossoming or blooming.*

*Matting* is more noticeable. It occurs when the tips of cut pile yarns untwist and fray, then get tangled with neighboring tufts. If the tufts untwist one-third of their length or more, and if the affected carpet is widespread and not a confined area subject to unusual usage, the carpet is generally considered defective if it is less than a year old.

Matting and untwisting happen because the *heat-set* of the yarn is weak. Plied yarns are put through a process that crimps the yarns, twists them, and then permanently sets the twist into the yarns. It is similar to a permanent wave for your hair. If the permanent doesn't "take," the curl won't stay in. If the heat-set is bad the twist will not remain in the yarns, either, and the carpet will pack down, looking old and worn.

Many mills have texture retention warranties to cover this condition. A standardized evaluation chart is used to determine if the complaint falls within the warranty (Figure 9-6). The warranty coverage varies from manufacturer to manufacturer and pattern to pattern from each mill. So check the details carefully. You get what you pay for. Cheaper carpets won't have this warranty. But the warranties are very specific, written by sharp legal counsel.

Here is a typical texture retention warranty. I have paraphrased it to keep it brief.

> During the ... warranty period, the surface pile of your
> carpet ... will not, under normal residential use, exhibit
> a significant loss of carpet pile texture, that results from

the carpet tufts bursting, blooming, opening or losing their twist and cannot be corrected.

Texture retention is the ability of carpet tufts to retain their visible shape ... and is measured by using an international standardized rating scale ranging from 5.0 (new or no change) to 1.0 (severe change).

Stairs are excluded. This warranty only applies to owner-occupied single family homes.

This carpet will maintain a texture rating of at least 3.0 for the first few years (depending on the manufacturer), and a texture rating of at least 2.5 for the remaining years of the warranty period.

Hot water extraction to refresh carpet texture, performed by a trained, qualified carpet care professional, is required at least every 24 months for coverage under this warranty. You must provide your receipts for proof of service.

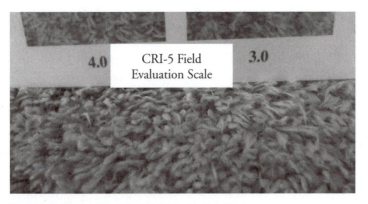

**Figure 9-6. Texture Retention Field Evaluation Scale used to determine texture change deviation.**

The warranty also specifies a minimum quality for carpet cushion. It excludes specific damages like cuts and burns. It also excludes changes in appearance due to crushing, soiling, shading, pile reversal, fading, and vacuum marks. The manufacturer also reserves the right to repair or replace the affected area of the carpet. This means that if the carpet runs from the family room, down a hall, and into the bedrooms, the mill has the right to only replace the family room if that one room contains the problem carpet. OK, you say. Well, if your carpet is 18 months old it has naturally faded somewhat. Then you put the new carpet, which is a different dye lot of the same color, against the old carpet. You will see a definite color difference between the new and the original pieces. You need to know that a partial replacement is a possibility.

## BLEEDING/CROCKING

Bleeding and crocking are two problems that refer to dye fastness. *Bleeding* refers to color loss from a wet carpet, either from cleaning or flooding. It is most common with darker shades, especially reds and blues, because large amounts of dyes are used to achieve the rich colors. Even when rinsed thoroughly at the mill, some excess dye residues can stay in the fabric. When you have your carpet cleaned, the technician (hopefully certified) should detect the condition during pre-cleaning tests. Then the technician will adjust the type of cleaning solution used to stop the bleeding. If the condition seems excessive, tests by the mill can determine if the bleeding is within tolerances.

*Crocking* means color rubs off when the carpet is dry. You might notice it when the soles of your white socks begin to turn the same color as your carpet. Or, if you have a dark carpet seamed next to a light color, the light area near the seam can darken. It is caused by improper dye penetration or dye fixation. Sometimes the condition is corrected by cleaning the carpet with an absorbent powder cleaner. If the color transfer is severe, the carpet must be replaced. Mills, however, do an excellent job of rinsing and fixing the dyes in the fabric. Bleeding/crocking problems are quite rare.

## CORNROWING

With *cornrowing*, cut pile carpet lays down in irregular rows ½ to 2 inches apart (Figure 9-7). This is a severe type of texture change. Most people think it is ugly. Cornrowing always runs across the traffic flow, but it even happens in little-used rooms that are only vacuumed. You'll sometimes see it when a door drags across the carpet pile. It usually happens with longer piles, more than ⅝ inch, and softer, fine denier yarns, especially low-density carpets with low gauge and stitch rates.

**Figure 9-7. Cornrowing.**

Despite years of research and testing, no one has figured out why some carpets cornrow and other don't. It is generally agreed that because the cut yarn ends can lay in any direction, it is also normal for cut pile fabrics to lay on their sides in rows. Furthermore, no one has discovered a way to remove this condition and prevent its return. A few mills will replace cornrowed carpeting as an accommodation. Most will not because they know that the replacement will probably cornrow, too. Why should a mill replace a carpet that is not defective? They did not mis-weave it or do anything else that caused the cornrowing.

Some people get extremely upset when their carpet cornrows, while others barely notice. It's just one of the things you must expect from a cut pile carpet. It happens with a minority of carpets. Not all cut piles do it, and it is impossible to tell which carpet will or will not cornrow. I have seen two rolls of identical carpets installed in two neighbor's homes. One carpet cornrowed; the other did not.

## SNAGS/SPROUTS

Snags and sprouts are tufts that have worked themselves up so that they are higher than the surrounding pile. *Snags* are face yarns, cut or loop, that have been pulled from the backing by something in the home. Snags are more common with loop piles. (Figure 9-8a). Vacuum cleaners with sharp corners or broken parts, pets, protruding nails from shoe heels, chair legs, and children can all pull out tufts and cause snags. Single snags should be clipped flush with the nap. If a row of loop pile has snagged and "zippered," a trained professional can retuft the missing row using scrap carpet.

Sprouts are more common with cut pile carpets. (Figure 9-8b). They are normal for new installations where loose tufts sometimes work their way out of the face pile. If the sprout has small blobs of latex (glue) anywhere along its length, it means that the sprout is not an extra tuft. It has either been pulled from the backing, or it has worked itself loose because of a weak tuft bind (discussed in the next paragraph). If you see sprouts around room perimeters, there is a very good chance that the sprouts are installation related. If the carpet is poorly made, even a normal installation can yank tufts when the carpet is stretched. However, stretching any carpet improperly can rip the primary backing and pull out tufts. A Certified Flooring Inspector can determine the cause of the perimeter sprouts.

**Figure 9-8a. Snags.**

**Figure 9-8b. Sprouts.**

*Tuft bind* is measured as the number of pounds of pull it takes to yank individual tufts from the carpet backing. Normal minimum tuft bind ranges from 3 pounds to 6 pounds, depending on the style and quality of the fabric. Three pounds might not sound like a lot, but it is more than enough for normal home use.

## WEAK TUFT BIND

When carpet yarns are tufted into the primary backing, they must be adhered to the backing or they will easily pull out. The tufts are glued to the backing with an adhesive compound using latex rubber as a binder. The general term for this compound is "latex." *Weak tuft bind* results from improper application of the latex or a mis-formulation of the latex compound.

The latex is applied using a roller the width of the carpet. Once the latex is applied, the carpet goes through an oven to cure the latex. Sometimes the roller that applies the latex to the primary backing puts on too thin a coat or skips an area and doesn't apply any at all. Eventually, the tufts in these weak areas work loose and holes appear in the face of the carpet.

If your new carpet develops a small hole because of skipped latex, a Certified Installer or Certified Inspector can easily re-tuft the hole, as long as you have a piece of scrap carpet.

## BUCKLING

*Buckling* occurs when a carpet loses its stretch and wrinkles develop (Figure 9-9). It can happen because of poor latexing, improper stretching, a soft pad, excess humidity, improper cleaning, or rolling furniture or equipment. Puckers around doorways and wrinkles in the traffic areas are sure signs of buckling.

### Poor Latexing

Just as poor latexing leads to weak tuft bind, it can cause a carpet to lose its stretch. Brittle, powdery, or thin latex will make a carpet too flexible and make it impossible to lay tight. If the latex application is not strong enough to bind the primary and secondary backings together, the carpet delaminates. Air gets trapped between the two layers and you'll see bubbles and buckles. When this happens along a seam, the seam opens up. You can stick your fingers between the two backings. When it happens in the center of the room, the carpet will bunch up when you vacuum. You can easily lift the carpet several inches from the floor.

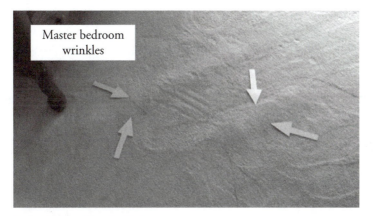

**Figure 9-9. Buckling/wrinkles.**

## Improper Stretching

A carpet is supposed to be stretched tight by using a power stretcher. Some installers try to save time and use only a knee kicker to attach the carpet to the tackstrip. This is the main reason carpets buckle. Emptying the rooms and restretching the carpet with a power stretcher removes the wrinkles. However, restretching can also change the location of cut-out areas like floor vents and doorways. These areas may need to be patched. Seams may also have to be remade. You're better off making sure the carpet is installed to industry standards the first time.

## Soft Pad

A soft pad may feel luxurious to you, but it is not good for the carpet. A soft pad allows an otherwise well-made and correctly installed carpet to flex and stretch too much. The carpet industry, working with the Carpet Cushion Council, has established minimum pad-thickness and density requirements for various types of carpet. Few retailers will sell you a too-soft cushion, but you need to know that the wrong underlayment creates problems.

Likewise, cushions dry out with age, especially rubber waffle cushions. When a pad turns to powder, the carpet loses its support and the carpet relaxes, buckles, and wrinkles.

### Excess Moisture

High humidity is bad for many types of floors. Carpets absorb excess moisture and relax, forming wrinkles. If the source of humidity is temporary, like immediately after carpet cleaning, the buckling should correct itself. If you live in an area with a lot of humidity, you'll need a dehumidifier to maintain a stable indoor environment.

Flooding or over-wetting from cleaning can make the carpet delaminate. Replacement is the only solution.

### Rolling Furniture

People don't realize it, but rolling a lot of furniture over carpet causes buckling. Heavy pieces with small wheels are bad for carpet. Using a wheelchair over a period of time can also create buckles. If you know the carpet will be subjected to wheeled use, discuss this with your retailer. The right pad for these conditions will prevent buckling and wrinkling.

## LINE FLAWS

All kinds of lines appear in carpets. You can see some as soon as the carpet is rolled out; some don't show up for several days or weeks. Some run lengthwise, others widthwise. Some can be removed, others can't. Following are the most common.

### High/Low Lines

Lengthwise *high* lines or high rows in tufted cut pile carpets show up for a couple of different reasons. Carpets are sheared during the finishing process to produce an even pile height and texture. The shearing blades are like a reel lawn mower that runs the width of the carpet. If the blades are nicked, the carpet pile running under the damaged area comes out higher than the rest of the pile. Improperly set tufting needles can insert a row or rows of yarn which are too long. This happens with both cut and loop patterns. Sometimes the final shearing for cut piles misses these high rows. Loop carpets aren't sheared, so the high rows stay in the roll until inspection.

Although carpet rolls go through an inspection at the mill, these types of high rows are almost impossible to spot until the carpet is installed and vacuumed. Some high lines run through the entire roll and there might be multiple lines running through the roll. They are normally sheared after installation.

*Low* lines or low rows are caused by improperly set tufting needles that pull the face yarns lower than the surrounding pile. These short rows look like grooves in both cut pile and loop fabrics. Low lines that are only a few inches long are usually re-tufted. Otherwise, the carpet will have to be replaced (Figure 9-10).

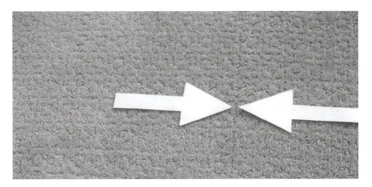

**Figure 9-10. Lengthwise low line.**

## Shear Streaks

You will see *shear streaks* when a tufting machine's shearing blades malfunction. The blades can jump up when the machine stops or starts suddenly. Then you'll see a widthwise band of high pile ½ to 1 inch wide across the roll. This type of band can be sheared by a Certified Flooring Inspector in your home to blend with the rest of the carpet.

Sometimes the blades move downward instead. Then you'll see a gouged widthwise band ½ to 1 inch wide across the carpet. This condition is not correctable. The carpet must be replaced.

## Stop Marks

*Stop marks* look like widthwise rows of missing yarn. The tufting needles are held by a needle bar. If the tufter stops with the needle bar in the up position, the empty primary backing can move forward slightly. When the machine starts, the needles insert yarn behind the empty portion of primary backing. With pile in front of and behind the empty backing, you'll see a line or gap. It is more obvious with a loop pile carpet.

## Shift Marks

Carpets are tufted with either straight rows or zig-zag rows. Zig-zag rows are made using a step-over stitch. When the tension of the tufting equipment is set too tightly, the carpet is made with too much tension. This tension appears as regularly alternating high and low widthwise bands called *shift marks*. Shift marks are visible in both loop and cut pile carpets. The bands are usually 2 inches apart and are not serviceable. The carpet must be replaced.

## Oil Streaks

Any mechanical equipment needs lubrication. Carpet tufters are complicated machines, with hundreds of moving parts that must be oiled. Machine oils from various places in the production line can get on the carpet pile. Part of the finishing process for broadloom carpets involves scouring and washing to remove contaminants. Still, because the oil is clear, you won't see it until it slowly attracts dirt and darkens. Then, after one to three weeks, a gray line, or lines, will slowly appear (Figure 9-11). You'll see this condition in usage areas first because the foot traffic brings dirt which sticks to the oil. In fact, the lines may appear to be intermittent or broken up because the non- traffic portions of the oil streak have not attracted dirt.

These lines will run lengthwise or widthwise, depending on what machinery part caused the oil to get on the carpet. Oil streaks show up more on lighter colors. Mills will send a professional cleaner to remove oil streaks. If a lot of lubricant is in the fiber, a streak may reappear, but it will be less noticeable after cleaning. A re-cleaning will remove any residual oil.

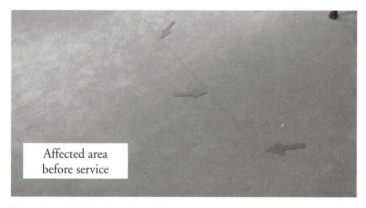

Affected area
before service

**Figure 9-11. Widthwise oil streak.**

## Pattern Bowing

This condition is only noticeable with printed or woven patterned carpet and loop patterned carpet. There are several causes for a crooked pattern, but the end result is that the pattern does not run straight when you look across or down the room.

It is possible that the installers stretched the carpet pattern unevenly and caused it to bow. It is also possible that the machinery was "off" during manufacturing and the pattern was made incorrectly. Whatever caused it, the bowed pattern will make the room look crooked (Figure 9-12). The industry tolerance is generally a 1 to 1½ percent allowance. That means up to 2 inches of bow across a 12-foot width! A good installer can compensate for up to a 1-inch deviation by carefully stretching less bowed sections more than areas with more bowing. But if the pattern is too far out of true, you'll need a replacement.

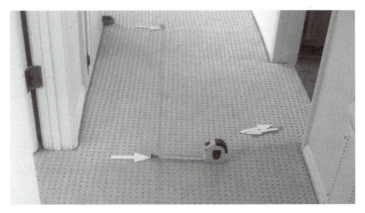

**Figure 9-12. Bowed pattern, off 1½ inches.**

## DELAMINATION

*Delamination* means the secondary backing separates from the primary backing and air gets between the two layers (Figure 9-13). This condition can be manufacturing, installation, maintenance or consumer related. The minimum standard for lamination strength is 2.5 pounds. Sometimes the latex compound formula has the wrong proportions. Then the glue will not cure properly. If it is too moist, the glue is weak. If it is too dry, normal traffic in your home turns the compound to powder; then the carpet will wrinkle and delaminate.

Thin latex makes the carpet feel soft before it delaminates. Getting a carpet too wet by improper cleaning or flooding also breaks down the latex. Spilling nail polish remover, oil, or other contaminants will cause delamination in small areas. Unsealed seams can cause a carpet to separate and delaminate along these cut edges.

As mentioned earlier, rolling furniture can make a carpet buckle. Excessive movement also delaminates a carpet. If you use a castored chair on carpet, you must use a chair pad underneath. Your weight and the chair wheels will delaminate the carpet in a short time.

Torn carpet weak lamination

**Figure 9-13. Weak lamination at seam.**

## SIDE MATCH

*Side match* is a condition that describes a color difference along a seam between two pieces of carpet from the same roll or the same dye lot (Figure 9-14a). Most of the time you will see a color variation along a side seam; that is, along the long seam in a room. Side match along a cross seam (end seam) is possible, but less likely.

There are two reasons for a color variation along a seam. The most common reason is due to pile crushing along the seam. Just as roll crush, or pile crush, can develop across the width of a carpet and make streaks, it can also occur along one side of the roll and cause a color variation along the length, making one side appear lighter than the other.

When the roll is cut and a piece of the darker side is seamed to the lighter side, there is an obvious color difference along that seam. It will appear that the nap of the two pieces are running in opposite directions, even when the carpeting is correctly installed. When viewed from one end of the room, one piece appears lighter than the other;

when seen from the opposite end of the room, the color of the two pieces reverses. What appeared light from the other direction now appears dark.

**Figure 9-14a. Side match.**

This color variation usually self-corrects through vacuuming and foot traffic. If it does not go away on its own, it can be removed the same way that roll crush marks are removed. Hand steaming and brushing a wool or nylon fabric will correct the lay of the pile and correct the apparent color difference. Edge crush is fairly common with cut pile carpets.

A carpet that is unevenly dyed across its width also creates a side-match condition when it is cut and seamed. Most carpet today is *continuous dyed*. After an undyed carpet is tufted and sheared, it passes under a dye bar that sprays color through small jets onto the carpet. These jets must be carefully calibrated so that they spray equal amounts of dye evenly across the width of carpet. Sometimes one edge of the carpet gets too much or too little color. When the installers cut the roll for seaming and place a light edge next to a dark edge, the color difference is very noticeable. The darker/lighter sides look darker/lighter when viewed from either end of the room. The color difference does not reverse the way a crushed edge reverses color. The industry uses a standardized scale to determine if the color difference is beyond tolerance (Figure 9-14b).

Many homeowners want a replacement right away. But wait: Do you really want your home disrupted again—furniture in the yard, unusable rooms—while waiting for the carpet to be inspected and then waiting again while a replacement carpet is ordered, shipped, and re-installed? Many Certified Inspectors are also trained color correctors. We can apply carpet dye to the light edge and blend the color difference so that it matches the correct factory color. The dyes we use are identical to factory dyes. They are colorfast and can be repeatedly cleaned. Side match correction, or color blending, could be a smart alternative to replacing the carpet. Besides, you have the final word. You must be happy with the work or you don't accept the results.

Figure 9-14b. Standardized Gray Scale used for determining side match deviation.

## STAINS/COLOR CHANGE: COLOR ADDITION OR COLOR REMOVAL

A *stain* is a spot that won't come out of a carpet. A stain is caused by either adding color to an area of the carpet or by removing color from an area of the carpet. Carpet warranties for stain-resistant carpet fibers are very specific regarding which types of stains are covered under the warranty and which types are not covered. Read your warranty carefully.

Everyone knows that if you spill bleach on a carpet, the color lightens and fades. Bleach, an *oxidizing agent,* is a color *remover.* Many other common household items also destroy color. Disinfectants, fade creams, pesticides, toilet and tile cleaners (Figure 9-15a), drain cleaner, oven cleaner, plant food, perfumes, and acne medicines (Figure 9-15b) all make stains by removing color from the carpet.

Some of these substances immediately ruin the carpet. Others, like fade cream and acne medicine, slowly lighten the carpet over a long period, sometimes months! Some of the worst offenders aren't thought of as bleaching agents. Little thought is given to removing them from the carpet when they are spilled. Try to keep all contaminants from spilling onto the carpet.

Strong, continual sunlight will also fade many carpet fibers, as well as furniture fabrics and paint (Figure 9-15c). If rooms in your home are subject to direct sunlight, you should consider one of the solution-dyed fibers. You should also think about tinted window glass and window coverings.

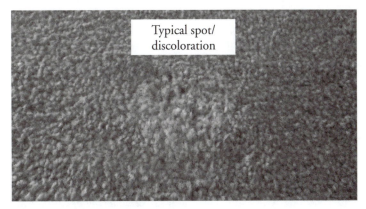

Typical spot/ discoloration

**Figure 9-15a. Chemical discoloration.**

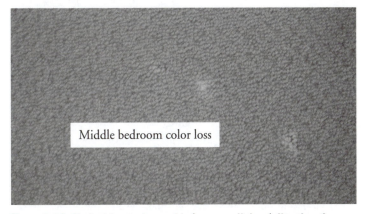

Middle bedroom color loss

**Figure 9-15b. Typical benzoyl peroxide (acne medicines) discoloration.**

**Figure 9-15c. Sun fading.**

*Reducing agents* change the carpet color by *adding* color. Common reducing agents are shoe polish, ink, furniture stain, mustard, chocolate, grass, vomit, and urine. Once these stain your carpet, even professional cleaners will have a hard time getting them completely out. They may lighten the stain, but there will be some discoloration of the carpet color.

## FILTRATION SOILING

If you have ever seen a carpet darken along a wall or stair edges where no one walks, you have noticed *filtration soiling*. When the ventilation system moves air through a house, the carpet acts as an air filter. Air flow deposits fine soil and dust along carpeted walls, stair edges, under frequently closed doors, and even subfloor joints. You may see black dots in the carpet around room edges. This is where knee kicker teeth have broken the secondary backing, air flows through these holes, and dust collects. Sometimes little-moved drapery hems touching the carpet or furniture skirts slow airflow enough to allow fine soil to outline the fabric onto the carpet. Filtration soiling is a function of the way the house is built.

What can you do about it? A Certified Carpet Cleaner can probably remove most of the discoloration, but the problem will slowly reappear when you run the ventilation system. It will take work, but you can pull up the carpet around room perimeters to caulk the space between the drywall and floor. On stairways, you'll need to caulk between the stairway frame and the staircase. Keep doors to unused rooms open.

If subfloor joints are allowing dust to collect in the carpet, you'll have to pull up the carpet, correct the subfloor, then re-stretch and clean the carpet. The object is to prevent airflow and dust collection.

## A FINAL THOUGHT

No machine-made carpet is perfect. They all have slight imperfections if examined closely enough. But manufacturers go to great lengths to make a carpet for you that is as close to perfect as possible. The problems listed here are rare. Do not think that they are found in every roll of carpet. The chances of having a problem are small. Buy the carpet you like and enjoy it. That's what life is about.

# 10

# MAKING A CLAIM

## "THE SQUEAKY WHEEL" OR EFFECTIVE COMPLAINING

What should you do if you are unhappy after the carpet is installed? What is the most effective way to get the retailer to listen to your problems? What is a reasonable length of time to allow someone to handle your complaint? And what should you expect when it comes to settling a claim?

Begin any complaint with your salesperson and work your way up the chain of command. Notify the dealer immediately if you are unhappy, or as soon as you notice the problem. (Some problems won't show up right away.) Your retailer wants you to be happy! Otherwise there won't be any referrals or repeat business from you.

Have the decorator, retailer, or independent professional carpet inspector come to your home as soon as possible to check the complaint. Some dealers handle complaints faster than others. Often the customer's attitude has a lot to do with the way a complaint is handled. Be as pleasant as possible when complaining, but be firm. The inspector will check the job to see if a problem exists with the carpet, the installation, or maintenance. Is it possible *you* have "buyer's remorse"?

An installation complaint, such as a poorly made seam, demands that the installer return to correct it. You can ask for a different installer if you feel the original one was incompetent or obnoxious. But the dealer usually tries to send back the same installer—who has already been paid—because it is the installer's responsibility to correctly install the carpet. The retailer would have to pay a second installer to correct the mistakes of the first one and will do everything possible to avoid any extra expense.

While it may seem odd for an installer to be able to correct what he couldn't do right the first time, most installers are good mechanics and can correct their own mistakes. There are rare occasions when an installation is done so badly that the only way to correct it is to take up the entire job and rework it. If this happens, you do have the final say as to whether the rework is acceptable or not.

Another possibility is that your complaint involves a misunderstanding of some type. Some possibilities are spot cleaning, maintenance, or unrealistic expectations regarding the carpet's performance. (Hopefully this won't happen, because you have read and understood this book.) Your salesperson will try to explain the situation and rectify the misunderstanding to your satisfaction. Keep an open mind and have faith in your salesperson.

If your complaint is with the carpet itself, things could get more complicated. The problem could be with what you perceive as a physical defect, or it could relate to the carpet's performance. Call the dealer and insist that someone look at the carpet. Be patient. You might have to wait a week for a visit. If the salesperson or store manager cannot explain the condition to your satisfaction, the mill representative (area salesperson) might get involved. Each carpet mill has its own policy regarding complaints. What follows is only a typical example. Your own experience may differ.

Keep in mind that mill reps have large territories and travel a lot. They usually have specific days set aside for visits to each account. This means that your complaint is not the only one the rep has on file. So it might take 2 to 6 weeks before the mill rep calls to make an appointment and another couple of weeks before he/she visits your home to look at the complaint. By this time, you have put all the furniture back in the rooms, set up the beds, and unpacked all the boxes with "small" stuff.

Let's assume that your complaint involves a manufacturing defect and the rep is knowledgeable enough to recognize it as correctable. The rep insists on sending someone to restore the carpet to first-quality standards. Mills reserve the right to correct a problem before they replace a carpet, just as an installer has the right to correct an installation problem. (If your new car has a scratched door, the car dealer paints the scratch rather than replacing the door or the car.) This is a lot easier than pulling up the entire job and putting you through a reinstallation. (Move everything outside again?!) Even if you don't believe that the service will correct the condition, be cooperative and allow the mill to try. You'll be amazed at what an expert serviceperson does to correct problems.

If your complaint can't be resolved through repair, the mill rep usually offers an adjustment. It is normally based on the wholesale cost of the carpet and the perceived severity of the problem. If the condition is visual (not something that will shorten the life of the carpet) and you can live with the looks of the carpet, consider an adjustment. Most mills first offer a credit of 10 to 20 percent. You can counter with a larger percentage, perhaps 30 to 40 percent. The maximum any mill ever offers is a 50-percent adjustment. Remember that if you accept an adjustment, the claim is closed, as far as the mill is concerned. The defect remains in the carpet after the credit is spent. The rest of the warranty should be unaffected.

If you feel an adjustment will not make you happy, you can insist on a replacement. The mill could request a certified, independent carpet inspector to evaluate the claim and make sure that the complaint is valid. Certified Flooring Inspectors are trained not only to recognize carpet defects and installation problems, but to service and correct these problems wherever possible. Inspectors are unbiased because they are not employees of the mill, dealer, or installer.

After examining your carpet and documenting the complaint with photographs, the inspector writes a report. The report evaluates the condition and determines if it is manufacturing, installation, or maintenance related. Most mills follow the inspector's evaluation. If the inspector thinks you have a valid non-serviceable complaint under the terms of the warranty, the claims department usually follows up with a replacement. If the inspector determines that the claim is not valid, the mill politely writes you to say that they are closing the claim.

If you qualify for a replacement, you receive an exact duplicate of your original purchase, including quality and color. Most mills do not allow the consumer to switch to a different carpet. Also, depending on the warranty and the reason for replacement, labor may or may not be covered.

Your retailer must supply the labor for any reinstallation and often receives no reimbursement from the mill. Some dealers replace the carpet at no additional cost to you. If you bought from a "mom and pop" store, your retailer may ask you to pay for the replacement labor, or to at least split the cost with them. This is something you might want to discuss when you initially buy the carpet. Then you won't have any surprises if a replacement is needed later. If you bought through an online dealer, you are responsible for the replacement labor.

What can you do when the mill denies your claim? The dealer could simply agree with the mill's decision and tell you that nothing more can be done. A dealer who values you as a customer could replace the carpet at dealer expense and negotiate with the mill later. This involves dealer risk because, besides the extra labor costs, the result could be a pile of used carpet in the dealer warehouse that the mill refuses to accept. But at least the dealer has a happy, satisfied customer who will tell friends about the wonderful service and who will return for another purchase.

When you have a carpet complaint, remember to be reasonable, cooperative, and patient. You are dealing with other human beings and, to use an old saying, you catch more flies with sugar than vinegar.

If you are sure that you have a valid complaint and both the mill and the retailer refuse to work with you, one more option is available to you: small claims court. You can find a Certified Carpet Inspector in your area using an Internet search. Armed with an inspection report that outlines the nature of the complaint and states who is responsible, you can go to court and talk directly to the judge. No attorneys are allowed. You can bring your Inspector as an expert on your behalf. It has been my experience that small claims courts are sympathetic to a consumer who has gone through a mill's claims process, has been turned down, but can prove a valid claim. It is a low-cost way for one last try at satisfaction.

# GLOSSARY

**Acclimation**—allowing a carpet to adjust to normal interior conditions before installation.

**Analogous color scheme**—a color scheme that uses two or more related colors in a room.

**Axminster**—a machine-woven carpet using unlimited colors. The tufts are woven through the back in a way that imitates hand knotting.

**Backing**—Kraftcord, cotton, jute, or synthetic materials used to form the back of the carpet. The weave of the Wilton loom forms the backing. Tufted carpet has two backings, the primary and secondary.

**Back seams**—made when the carpet is turned face down and cut from the back. They are generally less visible than face seams.

**BCF**—bulked continuous filament yarns. Any continuous filament yarn which has been crimped, bulked, curled, or otherwise treated in order to make the yarn feel bulkier.

**Beck**—a large container holding dye into which several rolls of unbacked carpet are placed.

**Berber**—woven or tufted looped carpet made from nubby plied looped yarns. Named after a North African tribe known for its loomed rugs.

**Binding**—a strip of cloth sewn over a raw edge to keep it from raveling. Binding is used when cutting carpet up to make into area rugs.

**Birdcage**—the end of a stair rail where the banister curves into a spiral.

**Bleeding**—occurs when a wet carpet loses color. This normally indicates defective dyeing.

**Bonded pad**—see *Rebond pad*.

**Broadloom**—carpet made wider than 54 inches. Broadloom used to indicate a high quality, but that designation is out of date. Carpet is generally available in 12-foot, 13-foot, 2-inch, and 15-foot widths. The wide widths allow fewer seams in large rooms.

**Brocade**—raised patterns created by heavy yarns on a background of thinner yarns.

**Buckles**—ridges or wrinkles that appear in a carpet after it is installed wall to wall. The condition is caused by either improper installation or faulty material.

**Bulking**—crimping or curling yarns to produce additional fullness.

**Bullnose**—a bottom step formed by extending the nosing (front edge) well over the riser. It's usually curved at the end and wider than the rest of the steps.

**Burling**—a carpet repair involving hand-tufting face yarns into any void area, either at the mill or after installation.

**Carpet**—a general term for fabrics used to cover flooring.

**Carved pile**—a patterned carpet made by shearing the pile at different levels.

**Cellulosic fibers**—rayon, acetate, and triacetate, all derived from wood. These fibers are not good for carpet yarns. Instead, non-cellulosic fibers made from chemicals are used for carpet yarns.

**Chain binders**—yarns running warpwise (lengthwise) in the back of a woven carpet. They bind all construction yarns together. The chain binders alternate over and under the weft (widthwise binding) and filling yarns, pulling the pile yarns down and the stuffer yarns up for a tight weave.

**Color family**—formed by mixing the primary colors; red/yellow, yellow/blue, and blue/red.

**Complementary color scheme**—uses contrasting colors for a room theme.

**Construction**—the process used to combine face yarns and backing fibers into a carpet. Refers to both woven and tufted carpet.

**Continuous filament**—synthetic yarn drawn from a liquid into a continuous length. It does not shed when spun into carpet yarn. Silk is the only natural continuous filament fiber.

**Cornrowing**—an effect produced when the carpet pile lays down in rows or grooves perpendicular to the traffic flow. The corrugated look can occur in any cut pile fabric. It is not a defect, although most people agree that it is unsightly. The exact cause is unknown, and there is no permanent method to correct it.

**Crab**—a hand tool used to install carpet in areas too small for a knee kicker.

**Creel**—a framework above a loom or tufting machine that feeds yarn to the weaving or tufting mechanism.

**Crimp**—a method used to create a bulkier yarn. This helps cover more carpet with less yarn and helps spun-staple yarns to better interlock.

**Crocking**—improperly dyed carpet in which the dye runs. With dry crocking, the color rubs off, often onto socks or clothing. Wet crocking (bleeding) is noticeable only when the fabric is wet.

**Cross seams**—seams made at the widthwise ends of carpet.

**Crushing**—normal, temporary flattening of carpet pile through use, especially noticeable with cut pile carpets. Vacuuming lifts the pile and corrects the crushing.

**Cushion**—see *Pad*.

**Cut pile**—all carpeting is made as loop pile. During the manufacturing process, knives cut the loops and form cut pile carpet.

**Delamination**—in tufted carpet, the separation of the primary and secondary backings.

**Delustering**—reducing the brightness of synthetic fibers through chemical means. This gives a more wool-like appearance.

**Denier**—the weight of 9,000 meters of silk filament, which equals one gram. Today, fiber denier describes the relative diameter of the filament. The higher the denier, the larger the diameter of the filament. Standard residential carpet fiber ranges from 16 to 18 denier per filament (DPF). The "soft hand" carpets use a low-denier fiber, 4 to 12 DPF.

**Differential dyes**—chemically structured to produce different color strengths on the same fiber.

**Differential dyeing fibers**—fibers treated so their affinity for dyes makes them accept more or less color.

**Drop match**—a pattern that repeats diagonally across the width of the carpet, with each pattern figure dropping a certain distance before repeating again. All patterned carpet must be matched at the seams.

**Dry cleaning**—a method of cleaning carpet by applying a dry substance impregnated with cleaning agents to the face pile. The dry compound is worked with brushes into the face pile, where it absorbs soil and is vacuumed up. Works best for touching up between hot-water extraction cleaning.

**Dye**—coloring or pigment used to color fibers, yarns, or carpets. Includes natural and synthetic pigments.

**Dyeing**—process of applying color to carpet face yarns. These are the most common methods:

*Beck/Piece* —up to 200 yards of tufted carpet are sewn into one piece and placed in a dye beck (tank). It is rotated through the hot dye until the correct color is achieved.

*Cationic*—a chemical that is added to the yarn, allowing it to react to dyes differently than untreated yarn. When tufted into a carpet at the same time, yarns can make three different colors from one batch of dye.

*Continuous*—as carpet moves continuously through a dye machine, dye is sprayed directly onto the carpet. The carpet continues to move into a steam chamber, where the dye is set.

*Resist*—treating carpet pile to resist and repel dye from specific areas to form a pattern.

*Skein*—the oldest dyeing method used in carpet manufacture. Skeins are single-yarn strands that are dyed before being plied into finished carpet yarns.

*Solution*—adding color to liquid synthetics before drawing into fibers, producing extremely colorfast yarns.

*Space*—dyeing long strands of continuous filament yarns several colors before tufting to create a tweed effect.

*Stock*—coloring large vats of staple fiber before it is spun into yarn.

**Dye lot**—several carpet rolls dyed from the same batch of dye. When more than one roll of carpet is needed for a large job, a roll from the same dye lot is selected so the colors will match.

**Embossed**—a pattern formed when heavy twisted tufts are used against a background of straight yarns to create an engraved appearance.

**Face seams**—seams made from the face instead of the back of the carpet. They generally are more visible than back seams.

**Face yarn**—carpet yarn inserted into a woven or tufted carpet. The face yarn is what you see when you look at a carpet.

**Fading**—loss of color due to strong light, chemicals, or gases.

**Fiber**—natural or synthetic strands of material used in making textiles, such as carpet.

**Filament**—a single continuous strand of fiber, natural (silk) or man-made.

**Filament yarn**—two or more continuous filaments twisted together.

**Fill piece**—a strip of carpet side-seamed to broadloom and used when the area to be carpeted is wider than the standard width of carpet.

**Filling yarn**—weft (widthwise) yarns used with the chain (warp) yarns to bind the face yarns to the backing yarns of woven carpets.

**Filtration**—a condition whereby the carpet acts as an air filter, trapping dust and particulates along a narrow space. Eventually, the affected area darkens from the built-up soil. Sometimes called atmospheric soiling.

**Flat sponge-rubber pad**—a flat carpet cushion made from natural or synthetic rubber. It is made in a variety of thicknesses and densities.

**Flocked**—a low-pile carpet made by adhering one end of the face yarns to a fabric using adhesive.

**Fluff**—lint or fuzz characteristic of new carpets. It is loose ends of face pile left after manufacture. Frequent vacuuming greatly reduces or stops the shedding.

**Frieze**—refers to both the short, tightly twisted yarns and the texture of carpet produced using the rough, nubby cut yarns. (Pronounced *free-ZAY*.)

**Frothed polyurethane pad**—a thin, dense foam attached directly to carpet backings; used mostly in commercial applications.

**Fuzzed**—the matted, stringy look after plied carpet yarns split or untwist.

**Gauge**—in tufted carpet, it is the distance between the rows of pile yarn and is measured in fractions of an inch. A ⅛-gauge fabric has eight rows per one inch section of width; a $^1/_{10}$ gauge has 10 rows per inch. It is the equivalent of pitch in woven goods.

**Greige goods**—undyed, tufted carpet without a secondary back. (Pronounced *GRAY goods*.)

**Grin**—a condition where the rows of face yarns separate to expose the carpet backing. Most common when carpet is installed over sharp edges, such as stairs.

**Gripper pins**—found on the underside of the knee-kicker and power-stretcher tools. These long, coarse, adjustable pins are used during installation to grip and slide cut pile and cut and loop pile carpet over the tackstrip.

**Hair and jute pad**—a felted carpet underlayment, or pad, made from a combination of animal hair and jute. The most firm of all pads.

**Hand**—the way a carpet feels when handled. Thickness, pile height, yarn texture, and backing stiffness all affect the hand.

**Hand-sewn seams**—a carpet seam made by hand, stitching two pieces of carpet together using waxed linen thread and a carpet needle. A latex rubber coat is usually applied over the stitching for added strength.

**Heat-set**—the applying of pressure, heat, and/or steam to plied yarns to set the twist. This keeps the yarns of cut pile carpets from fraying and untwisting and helps maintain the original appearance longer.

**Heddle**—on a power loom, a frame that holds warp yarns lengthwise, across which are drawn the weft yarns. The frame moves up and down to make an opening through which the shuttle passes with the weft yarn. This mechanical action is the same as the over-and-under movement of a hand loom.

**High-density foam**—foam pad with a minimum weight of 38 ounces per square yard and a minimum density of 17 pounds per cubic foot.

**High-low**—a textured carpet with more than one pile height, usually high and low loops or high cut pile with low loops (also known as cut-and-loop).

**Hot-melt seaming**—joining two pieces of carpet together using hot-melt tape. Seaming tape, a strip of special paper usually 6 inches wide that contains several rows of thermoplastic adhesive, is placed under the carpet in the center of the seam. A hot, flat seaming iron is placed under the carpet pieces and on top of the seaming tape. The iron is slowly moved over the adhesive, which melts. The carpet backing is carefully pressed into the melted adhesive. When the adhesive cools, the two carpet pieces have been seamed together.

**Hot-water extraction**—also called steam cleaning. A method of injecting into the carpet pile pressurized hot water mixed with a cleaning solution. Vacuum extraction removes most of the moisture and soil. When done properly, this is the safest and most effective way to clean synthetic wall-to-wall carpet. Most carpet manufacturers insist on periodic hot-water extraction cleaning to maintain their warranties.

**Hydrophobic fibers**—those fibers, such as olefin and polyester, that do not absorb water.

**Irregular**—see *Seconds*.

**Jacquard**—a mechanism on Wilton looms for making patterns. A cardboard roll with holes activates a selecting device that pulls the indicated face yarns to the surface. It works on the same principle as the music roll in a player piano.

**Jute**—a fiber derived from the hemp plant in India and the Far East. It is used in woven carpet for backing yarns. Jute is woven into sheets resembling burlap to form primary and secondary backings for tufted carpet. However, its use for tufted carpet backings has greatly fallen out of favor. Synthetic backings are used almost exclusively today.

**Kawasaki's syndrome**—this rare disease was once thought to have a link to carpet cleaning. Symptoms include fever, skin rash, and inflammation. The Centers for Disease Control has disproved any link to carpet cleaning. The Kawasaki Disease Foundation states that there is currently no accepted scientific evidence that Kawasaki's Disease is caused by carpet cleaning.

**Knee kicker**—a short device with gripper teeth on one end and a cushion on the other. It is used by installers to stretch carpet in small areas, like closets. It is also used to position the carpet onto the tackless strip before power stretching. The installer puts the teeth into the pile and bumps the padded end with the area just above the knee.

**Latent defect**—a condition that is invisible when the carpet is initially installed but shows up later.

**Latex**—a water-based emulsion of synthetic rubber and powder fillers used as a glue on carpet backings.

**Latexing**—the process of applying latex to a carpet backing. The latex locks in face yarns and acts as a glue when laminating a secondary backing.

**Level loop**—woven or tufted looped pile, with all the tufts the same height.

**Loom**—a device, hand or power driven, used to make fabric by crossing warp and weft yarns at right angles to form pile yarns attached to a backing.

**Loop pile**—woven or tufted pile of uncut loops.

**Luster**—the sheen or brightness of a carpet. Most fibers today are delustered to resemble wool. Duller fibers hide soil better.

**Matting**—a condition that exists when plied yarns untwist and become crushed, entangled, and fused. It occurs through normal use or because of a defective heat-set.

**Mill trial**—a carpet color or pattern which, while first quality, was not included in the current year's selection.

**Monochromatic color scheme**—a theme using one basic color in a room.

**Monofilament**—a single continuous strand of fiber. Fishing line is an example.

**Moresque**—a carpet texture produced by combining single strands of differently colored yarns to form one multicolored yarn end. It creates a salt and pepper look.

**Multifilament**—a yarn spun from many continuous filament strands. After texturing, they are called "Bulked Continuous Filament" yarns, or BCF.

**Nap**—the face yarns or pile of a carpet. The nap acquires a "lay" or direction as the carpet moves off the machinery and is wound into a roll.

**Nap gripper pins**—needle-like pins found on the underside of knee kickers and power stretchers. When the gripper pins are fully retracted, the nap gripper pins are exposed. Used to stretch loop pile carpets over the tackstrip pins.

**Needle-punched**—a carpet made by laying face yarns onto a backing material and using needles to punch in and lock the face yarns to the backing.

**Nosing**—the place where the top of a vertical stair riser meets the front of the horizontal stair tread.

**Nylon**—a synthetic fiber made from hydrocarbon compounds from the polyamide family. The Federal Trade Commission defines nylon thus: "A manufactured fiber in which the fiber forming substance is any long chain synthetic polyamide having recurring amide groups as an integral part of the polymer chain." The two main types are nylon 6.6 and nylon 6 carpet fiber. It is extruded from a solution through spinnerets (jets) into filaments. Nylon fiber accounts for about 65 percent of all tufted carpet made in this country.

**Olefin**—a synthetic fiber used in textiles, made from hydrocarbon compounds of the propylene family. It is made from chips that are melted, then extruded from a solution through spinnerets (jets) into filaments. The Federal Trade Commission defines olefin thus: "A manufactured fiber in which the fiber forming substance is any long chain synthetic polymer composed of at least 85 per cent by weight of propylene." The fiber is used in both indoor and outdoor carpeting, most famously in AstroTurf®. It actually makes up only a small percentage of total carpet sales. It is almost stain proof and cleans well.

**Oxidizing agent**—any chemical or contaminant that causes degradation to carpet color. Bleach and acne medicines are common oxidizing agents.

**Pad**—a cushion placed under carpet to prevent abrasion and provide softness. It is made from felted cattle hair, jute, wool, rubber, or foam.

**Pick**—weft (widthwise) yarns that run between the warp (lengthwise) yarns. The higher the pick number per inch of width, the tighter the weave.

**Pile**—the wear surface of a carpet made by the yarn ends of the carpet face or nap.

**Pile crush**—compression of pile thickness due to heavy traffic. It is normal for any carpet.

**Pile reversal**—see *Pooling*.

**Pile height**—the height of the face pile measured from the top of the backing to the tip of the pile.

**Pilling**—a condition where strands of the face fiber become entangled with one another, causing a rough surface similar to an old sweater. Pills should be clipped or sheared, never pulled, from the pile surface.

**Pitch**—in woven carpet, the number of warp (lengthwise) threads per 27-inch width of carpet. A higher pitch number indicates a closer weave. The thread count dates back to the days when 27-inch carpet was the standard width.

**Plied yarn**—two or more single yarns twisted together. Plied yarns are normally heat-set to keep the yarns twisted under heavy traffic. The ply number tells how many single ends are twisted together: two ply, three ply, etc.

**Plush**—a cut pile fabric style made from non-heat set singles spun yarn. It has a very smooth surface and is longer than a velvet design.

**Polyester**—a synthetic fiber made from long-chain hydrocarbons. Polyester chips are melted into a solution and extruded through a spinneret (jet) into filaments. The Federal Trade Commission defines polyester thus: "A manufactured fiber in which the fiber forming substance is any long chain synthetic polymer composed of at least 85 per cent by weight of an ester of a dihydric alcohol and terephthalic acid." Polyester is lightfast and very stain resistant. A variant polyester fiber is made from recycled soda bottles. It is known commonly as PET, or poly(ethylene terephthalate), and is a "green" form of polyester fiber. Another variant, made from PTT, is called Triexta. It is marketed by Mohawk Industries as Smartstrand.

**Pooling**—also called watermarking, shading, or pile reversal. Normal for cut pile fabrics, it is a dark, irregular area formed by the face pile reversing direction or laying on its side. Usually seen in a traffic area, the actual cause is unknown.

**Power head**—the motorized beater brush section of a canister (tank) type vacuum cleaner.

**Power stretcher**—a tool used to stretch a long section of carpet over a pad. It consists of a head with adjustable gripper teeth, tubular extensions, and a padded end. The padded end is placed against the wall opposite from the carpet to be stretched, with the tubes extended across the room and the gripper teeth in the pile. A lever attached to the head allows the installer to stretch the carpet using very little effort. This tool should be used in all rooms to assure proper stretch.

**Primary backing**—in tufted carpet, the woven or non-woven sheet into which the face yarns are tufted. It is made from polypropylene (olefin).

**Prime polyurethane pad**—also called prime urethane. It is made by combining liquid ingredients in a block form. The density of the finished foam is determined by the proportions of the chemicals and the cell size. Once the foam has cured, it is sliced into sheets.

**Primary colors**—the three colors from which all other colors are made: red, yellow, and blue.

**Printed carpet**—carpet with patterns applied using various printing systems.

**PTT—a type of polyester fiber:** see *Triexta.*

**Pucker**—a wrinkle in a seam caused by one side being longer or shorter than the other.

**Random sheared**—in looped carpet, a pattern made by shearing only some of the loops into cut pile. The looped areas look lighter than the sheared areas.

**Rebond pad**—a carpet underlayment made from recycled polyurethane foam scrap. It is easily recognized by its speckled color. It is available in a variety of thicknesses and densities.

**Reed**—in woven carpets, the comb-like device that pushes each weft (widthwise) row against the preceding one to ensure a tight fabric.

**Remnant**—the end of a carpet roll less than 9 feet long.

**Repeat**—in patterned carpet, the frequency and distance that the pattern recurs, measured lengthwise.

**Resilience**—the ability of a carpet to return to its original texture and thickness after being crushed by traffic or furniture.

**Restretch**—carpet stretching after the original installation to correct wrinkles or a loose fit. A power stretcher should be used whenever possible.

**Riser**—the vertical portion of a step.

**Roll crush**—pile distortion, usually in the form of widthwise bands or streaks, which can be found in any type or quality of carpet. Cut pile fabrics are more prone to roll crush. It is self correcting when the condition is slight. Only wool and nylon piles can be corrected by applying steam.

**Rotary shampooing**—see *Shampooing.*

**Round wire**—in woven carpet, the wire over which face yarns are drawn to form looped pile.

**Rug**—any loose-laid carpet.

**Saxony**—a cut pile made with plied, heat-set yarns with good tuft-tip definition. Saxonys are longer than plushes, although many people call smoother finished Saxonys plushes.

**Sculptured**—a patterned carpet made by using high and low, cut and looped yarns.

**Seam**—the area where two pieces of carpet are joined. *Side* seams join two pieces together at the long *sides* of the fabric. *Cross* seams join two pieces of carpet *across* the narrow ends of the carpet.

**Seam diagram**—a floor plan which shows the placement of all seams in a given installation. The end user should understand the seam diagram and approve it before installation begins.

**Seaming**—joining two pieces of carpet together permanently.

**Secondary backing**—the backing that is visible when a tufted carpet is turned over. It is made from woven or non-woven olefin. It is attached to the primary backing by a latex-based adhesive and adds stiffness and dimensional stability to the carpet.

**Seconds**—also called irregulars. Carpet that does not meet a manufacturer's first-quality standards because of off-quality defects ranging from color variation to poor backing lamination. Seconds may be an excellent value.

**Selvage (selvedge)**—the lengthwise, factory-finished edge portion of a carpet.

**Serging**—stitching heavy yarn around the edge of a carpet to prevent raveling.

**Shading**—a color difference in the carpet pile caused by yarn ends in one area laying in a different direction than the rest of the pile. Light reflecting off the sides of the yarn produces a lighter color than light which reflects off the yarn tips to make a darker color. Shading is normal and characteristic for all cut pile carpets. When severe, it is called watermarking or pooling.

**Shag**—a cut pile longer than ¾ inch, where the sides of the yarn form the wear surface.

**Shampooing**—the oldest method of carpet cleaning, utilizing a rotary brush to apply a shampoo solution to the carpet pile. Its main drawbacks are over-wetting and the residue that is left behind which causes the carpet to quickly resoil.

**Shearing**—the process in which the carpet is drawn under revolving cutting blades similar to a reel lawn mower, producing a smooth finish.

**Shedding**—a normal condition where loose fiber ends leftover from manufacturing work their way to the pile surface. Shedding subsides over a short time with vacuuming.

**Short roll**—a piece of carpet shorter than a full roll but longer than a remnant; usually 20 to 40 feet.

**Shot**—in woven carpets, the number of weft (widthwise) yarns in relation to each row of warp (lengthwise) pile yarns. A two-shot fabric has two weft yarns for each row of pile tufts. A three-shot fabric has three weft yarns for each row of pile tufts. More shots help make a heavier fabric.

**Shuttle**—the long, narrow device that carries the weft (widthwise) yarns across the loom when the heddle opens.

**Side match**—a color difference along a seam between two pieces of carpet from the same roll or dye run (lot). It is caused by pile crush or uneven dyeing.

**Side seams**—seams made along the lengthwise side of the carpet.

**Singles yarn**—one-ply face yarns used in velvet and plush constructions.

**Skein-dyed yarn**—see *Dyeing*.

**Snag**—face yarns pulled from the carpet backing.

**Soil retardant**—a chemical sprayed onto the carpet surface that slows the soiling rate and offers some protection against spills and stains. It can be applied to all types of carpet fibers. It does not make the carpet stain resistant or stain proof, and it is removed after several cleanings. On stain-resistant nylon carpets, it is applied in addition to the stain-resist treatment. Teflon® and Scotchgard are two well-known treatments.

**Solution dyed**—see *Dyeing*.

**Space dyed**—see *Dyeing*.

**Spinneret**—a device with a perforated head, similar to a showerhead, through which a liquid is extruded to form filaments.

**Spinning**—(1) The process where short-length staple fibers are made into long strands of yarn. (2) In synthetic fiber production, spinning is the extrusion of a liquid substance through a spinneret and the hardening of it into fibers. There are three types of spinning: wet, dry, and melt. *Wet spinning* extrudes fibers into a chemical bath, which hardens them. *Dry spinning* hardens the filament after extrusion by passing the fibers through solvent that has been evaporated in the air. *Melt spinning* is a process where the fiber-forming polymer chips are melted, extruded, and hardened by cooling. Nylon, polyester, and olefin are made this way.

**Spot remover**—a cleaning solution that physically or chemically removes foreign contamination from a carpet.

**Sprouts**—long ends of yarn that protrude above the pile surface and which were not removed during shearing. They should be cut with scissors, never pulled. Sprouting is a defect only if excessive and unserviceable.

**Staple yarn**—short lengths (3 to 8 inches) of fiber that are spun into yarn using a modified worsted system.

**Stay tacking**—temporarily nailing one section of a stretched carpet to hold it in place until the remainder is stretched into place. Used in large, especially commercial, installations.

**Steam cleaning**—see *Hot-water extraction.*

**Step**—the feel of a pad underfoot; a combination of tread and riser in a flight of stairs.

**Stepover stitch**—a tufted zig-zag lengthwise row of carpet face pile.

**Streak**—a lengthwise or widthwise mark in a carpet caused by uneven dye, uneven yarn thickness or height, machinery oil, shearing, or crushed yarns.

**Stuffer yarn**—in a woven carpet, extra yarn running lengthwise (warpwise) to increase the carpet's strength and stability.

**Tackstrip**—see *Tackless strip.*

**Tackless strip**—also called tackstrip. Thin wooden strips, prenailed with angled pins and fastened near the walls in a room, used to secure stretched carpet.

**Texture**—any surface effect that gives added interest to the pile more than that provided by the basic design or colorations. These include high and low yarns, brocading, shearing, yarn twist levels, and yarn thickness.

**Three-quarter goods**—before broadloom, the first looms (hand and powered) made carpet 27 inches wide (three quarters of a yard wide); these were joined to make wider widths. It does not indicate any level of quality.

**Tip shear**—a carpet pattern created by shearing loops so the pile is part cut and part uncut. Shearing produces a dappled effect and can be random or a definite pattern.

**Tone on tone**—a carpet pattern made by using two or more shades of the same color.

**Traffic patterns/lanes**—the main usage areas of an installation, and the wear patterns that develop from such use.

**Tread**—the horizontal part of a stair upon which the foot steps.

**Triexta**—the newest fiber name approved by the Federal Trade Commission in 2009 for a subclass of fibers made from poly (trimethylene terephthalate) (PTT). It has been established within the existing definition of "polyester." Sold by Mohawk® under their Smartstrand® brand.

**Tuft bind**—the amount of force, measured in pounds, needed to pull a tuft of yarn from the carpet backing. Acceptable strength varies according to construction methods.

**Tufting**—in carpeting, face yarns which are machine stitched by rows of needles into a backing material and secured by a coating of latex compound. Over 95 percent of all carpet sold in the U.S. is tufted. The tufting machines run at a much greater speed than weaving looms, thus lowering the price.

**Tufts**—the cut or uncut face pile of a carpet.

**Twist**—the number of turns per inch in the length of a carpet tuft, usually 4 to 6.

**Underlayment**—see *Pad.*

**Urethane pad**— see *Prime polyurethane pad.*

**Vacuum cleaner**—a machine that uses suction and airflow to remove dry soil from a carpet. Vacuums are made as uprights or canisters (tank type). Generally, upright vacuums are more efficient at removing soil from carpeting.

**Velvet**—(1) In woven carpet, a short pile carpet made on a velvet loom. It is the simplest of all carpet weaves and is made in solid colors. Woven with wires, a loop pile is formed when the wires are removed. A cut pile is made when knife blades on the ends of the wires cut the loops. (2) In tufted carpet, velvet refers to a pile texture. The short, dense pile is made with singles yarns and has a very smooth finish.

**Virgin wool**—as defined by the Wool Products Labeling Act, virgin wool or new wool has never been used or recycled from any spun, woven, knitted, felted, manufactured, or used product. Does not indicate any quality standard.

**Waffle pad**—a carpet cushion made from natural or synthetic rubber in a mold resembling a waffle iron. It is sold in a variety of weights.

**Warp**—the yarns running lengthwise in a woven fabric. They weave in the weft threads.

**Watermark**—a severe example of shading. The affected area appears dark and seems to have had a bucket of water poured on it. This is not a defect of cut pile carpet, although many people find the condition unsightly.

**Weaving**—a manufacturing technique whereby lengthwise and widthwise yarns are interlaced to form a carpet. Examples are velvet, Axminster, and Wilton weaves.

**Weft**—in woven carpet, the widthwise lines that weave in the warp threads and lock in the pile yarns.

**Wilton**—a type of carpet weave made on a loom using a series of perforated cards that automatically select different colors of yarn (from two to six) to form the design. While one color is raised, the others run through the center and back of the carpet.

**Wires**—metal strips inserted in the weaving shed in the Jacquard and Velvet weaves so that the surface yarns are bound down over them forming a loop of the proper height. Round wires are used in loop pile fabrics and the loops are left uncut as the wire is withdrawn. Flat wires with knife edges are used in Wilton, Velvet, and Saxony weaves and the loops are cut as the wire is withdrawn, producing a fabric with a plush finish. The number of wires to the inch lengthwise is an indication of quality.

**Wool**—the hair of sheep and the yarn spun from the fibers of the fleece.

**Woolen systems**—yarn that is spun from short fibers, either natural or synthetic, and then interlocked and twisted as much as possible during the spinning operation.

**Worsted system**—a method of spinning yarn from longer staple fiber that has been carded to lay the fibers parallel. The fibers are combed to remove shorter fibers, and are spun and twisted into yarn. The fibers stand up in a cut pile carpet and do not shed as much as short staple yarns made on the woolen system.

**Yarn**—a continuous strand spun from staple fibers or spun from continuous filaments used as carpet face pile.

# ABOUT THE AUTHOR

Ohio raised Glenn Revere graduated from Ohio State University with a B.A. in Anthropology in 1969. His first post-graduate job was with The May Company-Cleveland as an Assistant Buyer in the carpeting department. After receiving his training from a National carpet inspection company, Glenn moved to Denver, Colorado and began his career as a nationally recognized Carpet Inspector.

As the flooring field matured and changed, Glenn became a Certified Flooring Inspector with specialties in carpet, laminate, hardwood, and engineered flooring. He owned a carpet cleaning company for twenty years and is trained in carpet installation and repair. Glenn consults for individuals, manufacturers, and installers.

Glenn lives in San Diego, California. In addition to consulting, he enjoys skiing, swimming, tennis, and fishing.

# INDEX